"The Three Dimensions of Business Growth methodology is a remarkable path for achieving business potential that's aligned with our COPI process used in peer-to-peer groups. George provides tools that perfectly complement our mission of enhancing business value for our diverse membership."

—TINA CORNER STOLZ, Author of *Your Seat at the Table*,
CEO, LXCouncil.

"M&A professionals and growth advisors see firsthand the heartbreak that happens when a business tries to go to market when it hasn't done the hard work to get ready. Worst case, the deal fails or the company's risks mean the offer becomes deeply discounted, and the client is left with few good options. I've worked with George and the methodology detailed in this book—if you're committed to helping your clients sell and prosper, I strongly recommend you apply his powerful advice."

—STEVE DUKE, Certified M&A Professional, Business Exit Consultant,
Principal, Duke Business Advisors

THE
GROWTH-DRIVING
ADVISOR

THE
GROWTH-DRIVING
PROVEN STRATEGIES FOR
LEADING BUSINESSES FROM
STUCK TO BEST-IN-CLASS
ADVISOR

GEORGE SANDMANN

Forbes | Books

Published by Forbes Books, Charleston, South Carolina.
An imprint of Advantage Media Group.

Forbes Books is a registered trademark, and the Forbes Books colophon is a trademark of Forbes Media, LLC.

Printed in the United States of America.

10 9 8 7 6 5 4 3 2 1

ISBN: 978-1-64225-875-2 (Hardcover)
ISBN: 978-1-64225-874-5 (eBook)

Library of Congress Control Number: 2023911159

Cover & layout design by Lance Buckley.

Since 1917, Forbes has remained steadfast in its mission to serve as the defining voice of entrepreneurial capitalism. Forbes Books, launched in 2016 through a partnership with Advantage Media, furthers that aim by helping business and thought leaders bring their stories, passion, and knowledge to the forefront in custom books. Opinions expressed by Forbes Books authors are their own. To be considered for publication, please visit **books.Forbes.com**.

CONTENTS

PREFACE

There are 32.6 million private businesses in the United States, of which 7.8 million have payroll.[1] Of these, 560,000 have revenues from $2.5 million to $100 million. This is the middle market, in which businesses generate over $10 trillion[2] in annual revenues, almost 50 percent of US GDP. If ranked as a world economy, the middle market would be number three, larger than the GDP of Japan and Germany combined. Private businesses provide 44 percent of US jobs and 63 percent of new jobs.

The very spirit of independence that drives people to start and grow a private business can also become its Achilles' heel. These fiercely independent entrepreneurs *think* they are fine, that they've "got this." They don't. If you're a business advisor, I am preaching to the choir because you see it every day. You know that most businesses fail; of those that survive, nineteen in twenty cannot sell as they are currently run. The jump from the founding generation to subsequent ownership fails more often than it's successful. How do we help them?

1   Adam Grundy, "Three-Fourths of the Nation's Businesses Don't Have Paid Employees," United States Census Bureau, September 18, 2018, https://www.census.gov/library/stories/2018/09/three-fourths-nations-businesses-do-not-have-paid-employees.html.

2   Adam Hayes, "Middle Market Firm: Definition, Criteria, and How They Trade," Investopedia, May 17, 2022, https://www.investopedia.com/terms/m/middle-market.asp.

They need guidance to understand and improve their business's strategic capacity so that they can grow profits and attract capital.

> **The businesses that survive and thrive share a prevalent behavior: they identify their weaknesses and get help from the over one million business advisors in the US market.**

The businesses that survive and thrive share a prevalent behavior: they identify their weaknesses and get help from the over one million business advisors in the US market. Hiring an advisor replicates the behavior of public companies, who routinely hire outside advisors like EY and Boston Consulting Group to drive growth. And this begs the question: What if we can help more businesses connect with the advisory help they need to become well-run engines that produce predictable cash flow and predictable sustainable growth and maximize shareholder value?

Answering this question is why:

- Growth-Drive's *vision* is to help $1 trillion of middle-market businesses move in the three dimensions of business growth.

- Growth-Drive's *mission* is to invest business advisors with the knowledge, tools, and support they need to build a thriving advisory business helping middle-market businesses win; by delivering superior client results, advisors attract and retain new clients and drive the growth of our national economy.

- Growth-Drive's *strategy* is to help senior professionals build thriving advisory businesses by delivering client wins, helping them leave an indelible positive mark with every client they touch.

This book applies to privately held businesses at every stage and is especially relevant to advisors working with businesses with revenues from $2.5 million to $100 million. As of February 2022, there were 557,530 businesses in this market. Professionals call this the "lower middle market." I really don't like that term because it is an outside-in view of the business. If you're the CEO of a $2.5 million business, it feels big; there's nothing "lower" or "middle market" about it. I am one of them, and we are fiercely focused on growing revenues and making our businesses easier to run.

Businesses that will be the most receptive to the services detailed in this book have at least $2.5 million in annual gross revenue. Why? Because the CEO of a ~$1 million business typically views expenditures from their personal wallet's perspective: you're a hit to P&L. At $2.5 million, the CEO begins viewing outside expertise as an investment. The following is a breakdown of the US market:[3]

GROSS REVENUE RANGE		NUMBER OF BUSINESSES	% OF TOTAL	% OF TARGET MARKET
$10,000,000	$99,999,999	182,690	1.17%	32.77%
$5,000,000	$9,999,999	149,199	0.95%	26.76%
$2,500,000	$4,999,999	225,650	1.44%	40.47%
	Subtotal	**557,539**	**3.56%**	
$1,000,000	$2,499,999	556,639	3.55%	
$500,000	$999,999	808,940	5.16%	
$0.00	$500,000	13,752,036	87.73%	
	Subtotal	15,117,615	96.44%	
	Total	**15,675,154**		

---

3   "US Business Firmographics – Company Size," NAICS Association, accessed May 18, 2023, https://www.naics.com/business-lists/counts-by-company-size/.

Who is advising these businesses and their shareholders?

- 665,612 CPAs[4] in 89,680 firms with 0 percent annualized growth 2017–2022[5]

- 2,160,836[6] employees[7] in 1,121,512 management consulting firms with 9.1 percent annualized growth 2017–2022[8]

- 93,786 CFPs[9] in 146,794 firms with 5.9 percent annualized growth 2017–2022

What can we learn from this data? To promote growth and maintain relevance in the market, CPAs should consider diversifying their services, emphasizing the value they offer, and differentiating themselves from competitors. The growth of the consulting industry highlights the impact that incorporating management consulting services can have on the success of CPA firms. In the target middle market, the number of consulting firms exceeds the number of businesses by a 4:1 ratio. This underscores the importance of differentiating services and prioritizing customer satisfaction to ensure the success of *your* advisory business.

---

4   "How Many CPAs Are There?," NASBA, accessed May 18, 2023, https://nasba.org/licensure/howmanycpas/.

5   "Industry Market Research, Reports, and Statistics," IBISWorld, January 25, 2023, https://www.ibisworld.com/industry-statistics/number-of-businesses/accounting-services-united-states/.

6   "Industry Market Research, Reports, and Statistics," IBISWorld, January 31, 2023, https://www.ibisworld.com/industry-statistics/employment/management-consulting-united-states.

7   Unlike CPAs and CFPs, management consulting firms are not regulated, and there is no dominant certification, so total employees is used.

8   "Industry Market Research, Reports, and Statistics," IBISWorld, January 31, 2023, https://www.ibisworld.com/industry-statistics/number-of-businesses/management-consulting-united-states/.

9   "CFP® Professional Demographics," CFP Board, May 1, 2023, https://www.cfp.net/knowledge/reports-and-statistics/professional-demographics.

While there are approximately ninety-four thousand CFPs, only a small percentage of them (around five thousand) are certified to address specific business issues for business owners, including exit planning. Providing this service can set a firm apart and increase client retention. However, due to regulatory and compliance constraints, most of these exit-planning CFPs are unable to increase strategic capacity and are limited to providing advice rather than implementing solutions. They need professionals like you to help create high strategic capacity so that their clients can meet their wealth goals. And the national economy needs you because you know how to make businesses immortal.

WHY THIS BOOK IS IMPORTANT

It has been my great good fortune to have spent over a decade (capping a thirty-year career as an entrepreneur) in the middle of a vast spiderweb of business advisors, both as the leader of a tech company connecting operational excellence with business value and serving as leadership and faculty for the International Exit Planning Association and as faculty for the National Association of Certified Valuators & Analysts. During this time I've helped with thousands of cases from the perspectives of management consultants, business coaches, CPAs, valuators, M&A pros, private equity execs, certified financial planners, exit planners, and fractional CFOs. Our work together on thousands of client cases inspired the development of the three dimensions of business growth, a unified system for moving clients from their status quo to having predictable cash flow, predictable growth, and predictable equity value.

Throughout the book you'll hear the voices of several senior pros. Listen for them—they're very present in these pages. Ed Wandtke of Wandtke & Associates is an authority in many areas including valuation, exit planning, accounting, and more. Larry Prince of Prince Leadership is a specialist on strategy and senior leadership, as well as an amazing facilitator. Andy Weavill of TenXGrowth is a management consultant with encyclopedic knowledge, especially sharp on execution leadership. And Garth Tebay of GBQ is what fractional CFOs should aspire to be, with an unrivaled depth of knowledge on valuation, strategic accounting, and implementing flash reports. We are in their debt. Thank you.

You can't learn to ride a bicycle by reading a book, but you sure can learn a lot about bicycles. The goal of this book is to expand your knowledge about the forces and techniques you can use to increase client strategic capacity. Let's agree that building a thriving advisory business begins and ends with delivering killer client results, and this book is all about sharing what we've seen work.

So here's the big question: Do you want to build a thriving advisory business? Let's go.

BECOMING YOUR CLIENT'S GUIDE

Your Engagement Roles

After reading this chapter you will understand the importance of discovering your client's growth goal and uncover the emotional link or fuel critical to sustaining long-term commitment to strategic execution. You will also understand the three roles you can have in the engagement and why preparing a strategic growth project plan always focuses on execution.

Every engagement needs to start in the same place: with the end in mind. In the context of a long-term business advisory engagement, we need to start with the execution in mind. The challenge, of course, is that execution is often the most difficult phase of the engagement. It places the most demands on senior leadership's time, the money being invested in projects, outside advice, and new hires. Perhaps most importantly it requires investing patiently before any returns are seen.

> **Every engagement needs to start in the same place: with the end in mind.**

This long-term commitment needs to be sustained. And as with many things in life, emotion is the sustaining fuel. The question is, How do we create an emotional connection between the growth engagement and the CEO's long-term personal goals? The answer is to identify the growth goal through the growth conversation.

Linking the CEO's investment of time and treasure to their family's personal wealth is arguably the ultimate strategic plan. If you've ever had trouble helping a CEO understand the value of your services, imagine changing the conversation from business-goal centric to personal-wealth centric, with goals funded by the business. The business needs to be understood as a vehicle able to deliver personal wealth. This becomes the growth goal.

The growth goal is the profit and transferable value number that your client must reach in order for them to take care of their family, stakeholders, and community. The growth goal is bigger than a mere year-end target because focusing on a year-end target often fails to create the commitment, capacity, and momentum needed to stay on trajectory for sustained growth. The majority of businesses focus on revenue targets, and this is the reason they plateau. How often do you hear a client say, "We're stuck. We want to grow, but we can't seem to break through"? Identifying a growth goal, creating emotional commitment, and executing a strategic growth project plan moving in the three dimensions of business growth have a proven track record of getting businesses unstuck.

If you think about it, the focus needs to be on strategic doing. The purpose of the growth conversation is to create clarity and focus and to confirm the client's commitment to an accurately defined destination. Becoming your client's guide on this journey begins with a conversation to help them get on the road to growth, to create clarity, focus, and commitment, and to help them decide to invest in themselves and their business through you and your services.

The growth conversation is your vehicle to becoming a trusted advisor and confidant. Through the growth conversation, we are going to help the CEO do several important things. First, we are going to take whatever time is needed to make a deep discovery into the client's personal financial goals. In other words, what does the business mean in relation to them and their family? Second, we are going to help them understand the implications of not reaching this goal. Third, in the growth conversation, we are going to prove our value by delivering value. Fourth, through this deep discovery conversation, we are going to make the emotional connection between designing and executing a strategic growth project plan that moves them from their status quo to their growth goal.

In advising, everything starts with a plan. Plans can come in many forms, but the most important factor is that they are tracking operational health and performance using objectives and key results (OKRs). Best practice is that OKRs be discussed, so OKR-D is the better acronym. Take a second and ask, does your client have a plan? If not, why not? If so, there are still further questions to ask. Clients often think they have a growth plan, but in fact they have one of these:

- A budget, with no habit of using forecasts and actuals;

- An exit plan, with no clue how to execute or if the plan is even possible;

- A marketing plan that typically ignores the rest of the business engine;

- A strategic plan, often not a plan at all; equally often completely ignored by leadership as they manage the business day-to-day; or

- A personal wealth plan, with the business as an illiquid asset used as a "slug" that will magically be converted to AUM at an undefined future date.

Plans must be actionable in order to move a business from their status quo toward a defined destination. Strategic plans must be rigorous, with concrete steps to reach strongly defined objectives and key results. Key questions to ask the client at this early stage include the following:

- Where is the business going?
- How will it get there?
- What does success look like?
- Who is accountable?

YOUR ROLE(S) AS ADVISOR

In order to demystify the process of becoming your client's trusted guide, this chapter will introduce wisdom and key information to gaining their trust and priority. First, consider that there are three roles you, as an advisor, can play:

The Architect ←→ The General Contractor ←→ The Tradesperson

A gating exercise to help you focus on the work you truly want to do and define the work you don't is to decide what role you want to play in client engagements. The architect helps define the scope of what is to be built and the purpose the building will serve, analyzes materials available for construction, and then creates a blueprint or plan. The general contractor takes this plan and leads the project, converting the plan into reality. Tradespeople wield tools and specific expertise, completing various phases of the project.

THE ARCHITECT

The architect writes the plan and builds the blueprint for growth. As the architects, advisors can prepare a strategic growth project plan and deliver it to the client ready for execution. As the architect, you will lead the growth conversation to help your client clearly define their growth goal. You will analyze the business to understand what your client must do to get the success they want, and you will use this analysis as you create a strategic growth project plan. You will engage in strategic thinking by identifying the client's goal and strategic planning by creating the overall strategy or plan of action for the company.

THE GENERAL CONTRACTOR

Experience tells us that clients have a hard time maintaining execution momentum by themselves, which is why successful engagements need a general contractor. The general contractor (GC) is the growth driver and helps lead the engagement as the CEO's peer. The GC sets the tempo in meetings with the senior leadership team and holds them accountable to defined objectives and key results (OKRs) as they execute the plan and ultimately helps create a new reality.

General contractors are involved on a scale from quarterly or monthly touches to weekly work with the senior leadership team. Growing a business takes years of focus and commitment. This is why we always start with the growth conversation to make the emotional connection between your client's status quo and their dreams, providing the fuel needed to sustain the project through to success.

THE TRADESPERSON

The tradesperson brings subject matter expertise to the table. Such expertise could be leadership skills or financial reporting processes, or maybe you're a marketing guru. While it's tempting to bring specific expertise into an engagement, it's a potential rabbit hole that will consume valuable advisory time with lower-value work. This runs the risk of eroding your role as the key advisor and peer to the CEO, pigeonholing yourself because you are moving from acting strategically to acting tactically. For instance, an advisor decided to help a company with its bookkeeping because it was easier than outsourcing it, and internally the business was a mess. This took the advisor from a $500/hour engagement to a $50/hour value. The advisor's intention was to help, but he unwittingly knocked himself out of the role of general contractor.

As a tradesperson you are not only getting pulled into the weeds of daily tactical work, but you are also starting to deliver commoditized time as opposed to value-based time. Ask yourself whether your stronger talent is being a strategic advisor or a tactical consultant. By maintaining bright-line separation between the two, you will by and large insulate yourself from a phenomenon known as mission creep. This is when the client pulls you into the minutia of running the business rather than respecting your role as the advisor. Without distinct separation, you'll soon find yourself spending valuable hours working on issues outside of the engagement contract. When you think of this in terms of the value-based revenue model created for your advising practice, mission creep hits your firm's revenue and professional satisfaction, not to mention being the client's road to nowhere.[10]

The architect creates the plan, redesigning the business from its status quo into a well-oiled machine that can deliver the client's goals. Here, utilizing the growth-drive methodology, a goal-driven plan is drawn up. The design is built around one question: What goal must the business deliver? There are two types of goals. There are professional goals, such as "I want to grow gross annual revenues to $20 million a year." And there are personal goals: "I need to replace $480,000 a year in personal income and sell the business for enough to do this." A key consideration is to start the entire process by narrowly defining

---

10 Value-based billing for a project, as opposed to hourly billing.

the key business goal in both time and success metrics, enabling the design of a time-bound and goal-driven plan. Market data collected from over fifty thousand CEOs is telling:

- 62 percent of CEOs want *growth*, to grow the profits and cash flows of their business,

- 21 percent want *operational freedom*, to make their business easier to run,

- 17 percent of CEOs are *preparing to sell*, and

- 83 percent[11] discover they need to grow their transferable value in order to meet *personal* wealth goals.[12]

For many clients, especially those later in their careers, a larger amount of focus is on personal wealth goals and the business's ability to deliver those goals. This is the realm of equity value planning. Your long-term clients will at some point shift focus from professional to personal goals, with the business as the vehicle for achieving those goals. It's an inescapable demographic reality: most folks want to retire, or at least work on their own terms. They'll eventually need your help replacing their income.

How does this shift impact our work?

- Grow clients (62 percent) change their definition of what *grow* means, from growing profitable cash flow to growing maximum transferable value.

- Operational freedom clients (21 percent) begin wanting to improve their work/life balance and shift into creating predictable transferable value.

---

11   International Exit Planning Institute's BERI survey

12   Data generated using CoreValue Software

- Prepare-to-sell clients (17 percent) go through a cycle: they want to sell but discover that the business isn't worth enough, so they join our 62 percent "grow" crowd. Eventually they shift their focus back to selling the business.

Recognizing these shifts in priorities is an opportunity for you to remain relevant as objectives change. This underscores the need for you to invest the time at the beginning of the engagement to identify and confirm your client's ultimate growth goal and to circle back semiannually to confirm whether the goal has not shifted.

Re business advisor roles: Are you a one or a five? In the same way as you need to define very clearly what types of clients you want to work with—business revenues, headcount, industry, geographic location, CEO goals, etc.—it's critical that you decide your role. We discussed in general terms the roles of architect, general contractor, and tradesperson. Let's add some definition. Here's a quick perspective: **advisors guide, consultants do**. Your job as a business advisor is to guide the senior leaders, not to do the work for them.

Using a scale of one to five, with one being the lightest touch and five the deepest, here's a great framework for defining your happy place. Where do you want to play, one to five?

1. Connector: you may be a CFP, an M&A advisor, a marketing pro, or a CPA who works with business owners as part of your core business, and you want to help them, and you. You don't want to be the growth doer; you want to collaborate with a two or a three, typically as an advisor on nonoperational issues like personal wealth planning.

2. Architect: you want to have the growth conversation, analyze the business, and prepare a plan, but at most you want to "visit the job site" periodically to see how things are going.

You do not want to help with execution. Advisor guiding the increase in strategic capacity.

3. General Contractor: you have the plan under your arm, and you are holding the client's internal and external experts accountable to converting the plan into reality. Advisor guiding on accountability to goals and objectives.

4. Tradesperson: you are physically helping develop and implement internal processes; for example a CPA might rebuild the chart of accounts, recast the prior year's earnings, lead/do the bookkeeping, etc. You're in the weeds: Consultant.

5. Fractional: for all intents and purposes, you are a part-time employee of the business, with accountabilities and functioning as an integral member of the senior leadership team. Blended role, in large part consultant but delivering some advisory guidance.

THE GROWTH CONVERSATION

Many advisors do not want to be involved with the execution phase. But whether or not you will be the one holding the senior team accountable to executing the plan (the GC), as the architect you need to create a strategic growth project plan that can be executed. If not, you've wasted your client's time and money, and they will most decidedly not be a satisfied reference account.

GROWTH CONVERSATION PRINCIPLES

You need a set of principles, or rules of the road, which can guide the growth conversation. You'll learn to rely on these principles as you lead this critical conversation, which right from the get-go is delivering real value to your client. Value because your client will leave each discussion with a better understanding of their business and personal drivers and will clearly understand you as their guide. These revelations cement your role, and the sooner you deliver valuable knowledge to your client the better. They should leave every conversation with you having learned something.

To make sure your client learns from every conversation, you need a plan. The plan is based on principles. The principles guide the questions you must ask patiently, questions that make sure your proposed actions are aimed at the correct destination. For example, if your client tells you they want to grow profits to $5 million within three years, the goal seems clear. But is it? Why $5 million? Why three years? Without asking these basic questions, you can completely miss the mark. You see, this client wants to get to $5 million in three years because they plan on selling the business and retiring, and they assume that they can get a 6X multiple of earnings at the deal table. Now odds are that they can't. Further, growing to $5 million might be at a rate of growth that outstrips their cash flow. And imagine if three years puts the business sale squarely in the depths of a recession. How will that impact the sale price?

The mindset that the growth conversation creates is actually as important as your advice because it opens your client's mind. Here are the core principles for leading a successful growth conversation:

- Transformational Mindset
- Question Everything[13]
- Deep Listening
- Advisor Silence
- Give No Advice

---

13   Daniel Coyle, *The Culture Code: The Secrets of Highly Successful Groups* (New York: Bantam, 2018).

- Client Self-Discovery

A transformational mindset is the first principle necessary to the initial growth conversation because as the trusted advisor, you do not deliver transactional services or products. You deliver transformational services. Questions guided by a transformational mindset discover all possible outcomes for a given scenario and work backward from each of these, building skills, flexibility, and agility within the competitive environment. A transformative mindset does not hurry toward some defined destination. Transformation is not a process, but a way of existing with constant mind paid to the macro and micro forces affecting a given client.

It starts by building trust. Trust is the glue for commitment. The growth conversation is designed to create and deepen trust, and looks like this:[14]

Result of the Growth Conversation: Commitment to Action

Willingness to Commit to an Ongoing Relationship

Personal and Professional Goals:
Trust with Sensitive Financial Information

FORD and Trust with
Personal Information

Awareness and Preference
over Other Options

Baseline Relevance Creates
Trust That Needs
Can Be Met

Low Trust. No Commitment to Action

14   Adapted from Maslow hierarchy of needs and https://www.nngroup.com/articles/commitment-levels.

If you're opening a conversation with a client and have been referred in, you have a small leg up on trust because you're cashing in on the trust credit from the person who referred you. But don't take it for granted; you need to get much deeper in order to create the trust needed for your client to share their ultimate why and to tap into the emotion needed to fuel commitment over the long term.

This is an "asking" conversation not a "telling" conversation. By approaching questions without preconceptions, practicing deep listening and focusing on asking questions rather than on delivering advice, you are creating a space in which your client can share freely. One of our advisors was called in to talk with a business owner interested in selling her company. She had started the process herself. The advisor began with a simple question, "Why sell?" Over the next seventy-five minutes, he only asked questions. By the end, she realized three things: 1) She did not know how to sell the business; 2) she no longer wanted to sell the business; and 3) had she decided to sell, she probably would have undersold the business.

Deep listening means just what the name suggests: listen to what is said, listen for what is not said, and never assume you know what lies ahead. As you've probably experienced during your career, these conversations can often veer in surprising directions. You must listen, not to reply but to learn. You are leading a conversation of self-discovery. Deep listening requires a temporary suspension of judgment coinciding with a willingness to receive information—whether that information be positive, negative, or neutral. Very often, as an advisor playing the architect role, it's not the direct content of what your client is saying that's most important, but drawing meaning from behind the

> **Listen to what is said, listen for what is not said, and never assume you know what lies ahead.**

client's words. For example, your client might say, "I need to grow profits to $5 million," but the key is understanding "Why?" Over time your questions deliver self-discovery, and a reciprocal relationship will emerge, with you and your client knowing, liking, and trusting each other.

Another tool you should apply liberally in these initial growth conversations is silence. Oftentimes you will ask your client a question, and they won't answer immediately. As the advisor and conversation leader, you may feel the need to jump in and fill the awkward-feeling silence. Do not. Silence is OK. Allow the silence to linger because the client is likely thinking deeply about the question you've asked. Prior to biasing them with your thoughts, allow them to articulate their own to see where they sit prior to your advice. The overwhelming majority of the time, they will eventually fill the silence and more often than not with a golden nugget of information.

Write this down at the top of your pad. In this conversation there will be no telling the client what it is they need to do, nor telling them where they need to go. Instead you're helping them self-identify what their goal is and how they wish to proceed.

Through the growth conversation you begin educating the client about the path that will transform their world from their current position (status quo) toward their goal. Ultimately you are their guide to successfully identifying a transformational goal, utilizing your curiosity and skeptical mindset to question everything and leave no assumption unchallenged.

Always remember that principles become reality through behavior and action (methodology and process).

GROWTH CONVERSATION METHODOLOGY

Now let's move from the growth conversation principles to the methodology. A methodology is an approach to converting principles into reality with a defined set of guidelines, techniques, deliverables, and processes.

The methodology steps include:

- Establish a Connection
- Set the Agenda
- Explore Where They Want to Go
- Identify Their Growth Dimension
- Discuss Their Why

The methodology uncovers the growth intent of a client, laying the emotional connection between professional and personal goals. When these goals are closely tied together, we get commitment to professional goals based on motivating personal desires. And this is exactly the client you'd want to work with, one who is completely committed and willing to invest time and treasure into reaching their goal over the long haul.

Your professional value is validated by successfully leading the conversation to eventually uncover emotionally important goals and identifying a set of principles—the three dimensions of business growth—that can be used to achieve the growth goal. Always remember, clarity is one of the client's biggest returns on investment from working with you. With clarity comes a realization that, whatever the goal, not only is it achievable, but you are the right person to lead the mission. The approach outlined here is effective because you are proving that you can help not by telling, but by showing. Through employing this methodology, you are delivering immediate value in the form of awareness, clarity, and focus.

Oftentimes a CEO is too busy within the whirlwind of their job to spend critical time on business analysis. They may think their goal and plan to achieve it are crystal clear. But they have not done any deep discovery to confirm the accuracy of the goal or the plan. I will give you an example. At an initial meeting with an advisor, the CEO threw up the company's initiatives on a whiteboard. By the end of the meeting, these initiatives had completely flipped—number one was suddenly number six and vice versa. The growth conversation clarifies both the direction and the motivation of the goal, further cementing client commitment to you as their trusted advisor.

Be sure to acknowledge where they are now and the client's success up to the point of your engagement. They'll appreciate you for this, and it shows that you fully understand what the potentialities are in terms of achieving their growth vision.

The next stage of discovery will include questions such as:

- What's stopping you from getting where you want to go?

- What stopped you from starting your growth journey earlier?

- What are the challenges?

- What are the obstacles?

- What fears do you have around taking the step toward growth?

You'll need to continue probing with deep questions, helping the client to uncover the various challenges and blockages to their growth.

Further questions might include:

- Why is growing a business challenging for you?

- Why do you think you haven't solved this particular problem yet?

- What's the impact of this challenge?

Clarifying questions might include:

- And what happens if you don't?

- What is the cost of not moving forward?

- Are there other alternatives?

Through this type of deep self-critical thinking, the client will clearly identify their barrier(s) to growth. Confirming that you and the client have clarity on the growth blocks is critical to starting the growth journey on steady footing. Having done this, you will simply reiterate the goal and help them identify the consequences of not reaching their goal.

Why? is a strong question and as you will find throughout the book central to your role as advisor. It's also the most powerful question your client CEOs will use in execution leadership. One "why" question that may seem basic but is quite illuminating is, Why do you want to achieve this growth? Their explanation reveals the motivation for investing in this project. But the first time you ask, the client will likely present an intellectual rather than emotional answer. If time permits, you should ask for their why multiple times to uncover the client's emotional motivation. Keep digging. Emotional drivers keep clients committed to their vision, whether they are driven by creating a better life for their family, establishing business immortality for future generations, honoring a hardworking relative or role model, or any other motivating factor that's deeply emotional. Emotion is the fuel for commitment, for sustaining effort over years.

After you have led the potential client through a deep analysis, it is a great time for you and the client to exchange feedback. Specifically you should cite both the most and least valuable parts of the conversation to streamline future meetings. Clients often report that they've never thought about some of the topics covered and that the conversation has provided some new ideas and food for thought. These questions will help the client clarify that the status quo is not an option. If they don't commit to moving forward on the growth journey and fully engage in the process with you, their business could suffer.

GROWTH CONVERSATION PROCESS

There is, of course, a process for applying the growth conversation methodology. Thus far we have covered the principles and methodology used to gain client trust and move an engagement forward. Think of the process as the playbook on how you'll run the conversation. The process is a well-defined set of steps and decision points for executing the methodology. The growth conversation will take as long as it takes. Do not try to shoehorn it into an hour; it needs to run its natural course. Some growth conversations take an hour, some two, and others run longer. Set a minimum time and always add a buffer in case the meeting runs long.

Before the meeting, research your client's background, professional accomplishments, and key mutual relationships via online searches and by reaching out to friends and colleagues. Having a general sense of your client's journey to this point lays a foundation for the meeting. You are not a private investigator—you are simply getting high-level, publicly available information in order to promote conversation flow. This information can uncover mutuality and catalysts to spark connections. People are social; they would rather do business with individuals they actually enjoy and connect with. People trust those they know and like.

The five key components of the growth conversation process are:

- Establish a Connection

- Set the Agenda

- Explore the Growth Intent

- Describe the Road Map to Growth

- Prove You Can Help Them by Helping Them

You begin to build rapport with your client by establishing some commonality and building a human connection between the advisor and the client. Establishing rapport is critical to molding the client relationship to the point where the client knows, likes, and trusts you. By establishing this connection, you show that you care for the client's well-being, remaining present as a helper and guide. Further you foster a key mindset—that this engagement is about the client. They are in control of their own growth goal, and through the growth conversation, you have pinpointed a growth goal to which your client is deeply and personally connected.

During the first phase of the meeting, spend a couple of minutes sharing what you know about your client and their business. Assure the client that all information shared will remain confidential. Next, invest ten to twenty minutes creating a vulnerable, sharing mindset. One approach is the FORD technique, an acronym for Family, Occupation, Recreation, and Dreams.[15] To use this technique, ask four questions on each of these in turn, following up on the most passionate answer paths. Listen deeply and avoid the tendency to "me too." There is only one hero in this conversation: your client.

Having established a connection, the next stage of the conversation is to follow your agenda. When designing the agenda, there is a balance between guiding the conversation and being overcontrolling. In addition to discovering their ultimate why, you want to learn about the business processes and results, the senior leadership team, and the current strategic capacity. The client will be comfortable having a conversation governed by an agenda where they have input and know what to expect. Describe the agenda aloud and then ask, "Is this agenda OK

---

15   I first learned about FORD and how to use it during the Certified Peer Group Moderator training with LXCouncil. Founder and CEO Tina Corner Stolz relies on this technique in her work, and it is incredibly easy and effective in a variety of personal, social, and professional settings.

with you? Is there anything you are hoping we'll cover that I didn't include?" This creates agreement on how to use the balance of time.

After getting permission to share the agenda, you can add, "Look, pitch in, please. If you have any questions or want to take the conversation a different way, please do." Or you might say, "I'd love to get started. I'd like to share with you an agenda for our conversation that I have found to be extremely effective. Can I share it with you?" Inevitably, the client will say yes, giving you permission to lead them through the rest of the discovery conversation.

By setting the agenda, you have also established that you will be the person leading what happens during the conversation. At the same time, you want them to feel the freedom to discuss and interject things they feel are important. The agenda should include discoveries that will uncover goals for the business over the next three to five years. Guide the client through a conversation that paints a picture of their current situation, their goal, and the obstacles along the way. Toward the end of the discussion, you should ask questions directed at removing any doubts they may have in terms of engaging further with you. The agenda clearly outlines what to expect during the initial conversation.

Having explained confidentiality and invested time in a FORD discovery conversation, clients should be comfortable enough to talk honestly and at length. Transforming the business should be innately exciting to them and aid in revealing their deeply rooted passions. Many clients are thinking about the future long before they meet with you, so this exercise affords them the opportunity to dig deeply with your input and further open up their thought process to reform.

The next part of the conversation is critical. When you explore where they want to go, there are many opening questions. One excellent option is: "If we were having this conversation three years from today, and you were looking back over those years to today, what has to have happened in your life, both personally and in your business, during that period for you to be happy with your progress?" Then be silent. Listen. This question enables you to get into the head and psyche of the prospective client and learn about them, their values, and what matters to them. Ultimately you begin the process of learning where they want to go in terms of growing the business.

As you continue start identifying growth goals by asking the following question, remembering to listen deeply and ask open-ended follow-up questions: What is motivating you to invest time in meeting with me? Your client may tell you they are meeting with you based on another advisor's recommendation, prompting you to ask, "In what context?" Your client shares a revenue goal, and you confirm it. "You've said you want to grow revenues to $25 million." You then ask, "Why is this number important?" Confirm salient points by repeating them and asking if you understand correctly, and once you are confident in your understanding of the client's goal, ask them, "What happens if you don't reach it?" Remember to listen deeply to the answer, as you will be uncovering another layer of the client's thought process. Do not hurry this part of the conversation; take time to let all discussion points fully play out.

From here on, you simply need to practice deep listening and ask supporting questions, such as:

- What specifically do you mean by that?
- What would that look like?
- What are you seeing in three or five years?
- What does the business look like?
- How many people will you have?
- What's the revenue?
- What's the profit?

With these questions, you're helping your client create a clear vision of the future. If your client isn't forthcoming with answers, you can try big, open questions to jump-start your discovery. Some great supporting questions include:

- What else can you tell me about that?

- What do you mean by ...?

- Tell me more.

- What exactly would that look like?

- What exactly would you be doing?

- How important is this result to you?

- How important is it that you achieve this level of revenue or profitability?

- What happens if you don't?

As the conversation unfolds, you will go deeper into the reality of the enterprise, layer by layer, asking supporting questions, and your client will gain more clarity concerning where they want to lead their business over the next three to five years. You will have uncovered a large volume of information about the business and the owner by the end of this conversation.

This leads to sharing the road map for closing the gap between their status quo and their aspirational future. We are not talking here about presenting concrete action steps—that would be completely inappropriate since we haven't completed discovery. But this is a great time to start introducing concepts like the three dimensions of business growth. When introducing concepts or giving advice, it's a great idea to create mindshare by asking for permission. Start with a question like: Can I share my insights on how you might achieve the growth that you want? Although you're controlling the agenda (as will be discussed in more detail shortly), you are also sharing control with the client, which builds a trusting, positive relationship. Final note: never forget good stagecraft. Ask yourself if the better venue for this discussion is your client's office, your office, a Starbucks, or over a white linen lunch.

FINDING YOUR CLIENT

What would a book on strategy be without quoting Sun Tzu, author of *The Art of War*? Sun Tzu tells us we must: 1) know ourselves; 2) know the enemy; and 3) know the terrain. Even with an initial understanding of the client's goal and motivation, you still don't have clarity on the details of your role as their trusted advisor. This is because you do not yet have firsthand knowledge of the terrain, a.k.a. the reality on the ground inside the business. This is your call to action. Say, "Jane, I only work with clients where I am confident they will earn a high return on investment from the work we do together. To see if this is the case here, we need to have a better understanding of what is going on inside your business. Does this sound like a good next step?"

At this point ask yourself, on a scale of one to ten, if you sense that the client is truly committed to growth. If they have identified their growth goal, which may be an evolution of the reason they gave you the meeting in the first place, and have verbalized the implications of not reaching the goal, you can start focusing on motivation.

By now you and the client will know if you want to work together, and if so, you'll need to transition to identifying the next steps. Be specific about the growth process and the journey on which you'll embark together. Once you have shared the road map, you are ready to share the objectives and key results needed to reach the growth goal.

For example, you could share a sample engagement timeline, which will be discussed in chapter 2. Best practice is to have two alternative approaches so that through your conversation, the client can review options and then clearly clarify and identify which is the best to embark on with you as their advisor. This can be presented simply on a single page.

Cement credibility and authority by sharing a case study of your work or of the growth-drive methodology in action.[16] A great case study provides social proof that you know what you're doing and that you know what you are talking about, so look for cases that you think will be relevant to this client. Close this section of the conversation by asking if there are any questions about what has been discussed so far.

> **Cement credibility and authority by sharing a case study of your work or of the growth-drive methodology in action.**

Inevitably, they will ask, "What does working with you cost?" Your goal is to use the information learned so far as a lever to change your client's mindset from cost to investment. You've done a great job with the growth conversation. You and your client have identified the potential growing pains and the impact that reaching their goal will have on revenues, transferable value, and their personal world. You cannot duck sharing your fees, but they should be presented in the context of the engagement. "Jane, if I understand correctly, you need to move your business from $2.5 million to $5 million, while also making sure the business can deliver $30 million of gross value. Is this correct? So you need to add $25 million to what the business is worth today, is that right? Does the outline of the work we reviewed make sense to you? My fee structure is simple." Then you can explain what they'll need to invest to analyze the

---

16   Cases are available for free by visiting https://www.growth-drive.com/cases.

business and convert the analysis into a strategic growth project plan. Explain that once you've delivered the plan, they'll have three options: implement the plan themselves, hire you to guide the senior team as it executes the plan, or hire someone else to help with execution.

If all goes according to plan, you can quickly move past this to the next phase: the action phase. You need to get them to "Yes!" so think about de-risking the client's decision by providing a guarantee of some sort. Common de-risking techniques include:

- No term commitment: "We will work together on a month-by-month basis, and I'll keep working with you so long as you are seeing results."

- Rolling the risk forward: Start by working together on a short-term, defined project like analyzing the business to uncover bottlenecks to growth, and if they decide to hire you long term, you will apply the project fee as a monthly discount on a pro-rata basis over the first year of the engagement. For example, if the project fee is $12,000, you will discount your $5,000 monthly retainer by $1,000 during the first twelve months.

Providing a compelling reason to say yes by offering people the opportunity of minimizing the risk of engaging with you is fantastic. Now you've taken the time-and-treasure equation and reduced it to time only because in their mind they're thinking if they don't want to work with you, then they're not really risking anything financially. Experience tells us that you will seldom be asked to honor this guarantee, and with this mindset, you'll often tip the balance and sell them on the engagement.

Always help your clients understand their return on investment from your services in terms of profits and value. Once they understand the profit-value equation, you can emphasize your ability to grow the value of a business by two-, six-, or tenfold. You can bring the client to value your services as an investment rather than a hit to their P&L.

As consultants, even if the initial energy and desire by that business owner to begin the process is there, we need to always reinforce their why by having check-ins with them emotionally, not just on the business but to understand where they are and where their management team is in the change management process and show progress. The hard data can also help reinforce their why and motivation to sustain them through the growth phases.

Be careful to only invest your time with clients capable of generating a strong return on their investment of time and treasure in a profit- and value-growth project. You will only know if the client will generate a high return on investment (ROI), and if this engagement is one in which you can be successful by gaining clarity about what the client needs to do to reach their definition of success. As discussed in chapter 3, clarity can only come from a deep analysis of the client's business.

THE GROWTH GOAL AND GOAL-DRIVEN DESIGN

The growth goal is always a dollar amount, and it is always a waypoint on the road to a bigger destination. Your client may think of the goal as their destination, and maybe it is. But if we agree that the ultimate measure of business success is high transferable value, then someone will be setting a new growth goal after our client has left the business—and leave it they must one way or another. Your growth conversation ideally uncovers how much cash your client needs to fund their long-term wealth plan; this cash can come from a variety of sources including distributions and sale. The growth goal can be communicated as a waypoint: "Once we've grown the business to $2.5 million in profit, we'll look at your options." Bottom line: when a CEO tells us they want to reach $2.5 million in profit, we need to make sure we are crystal clear on why that number and when it needs to be reached.

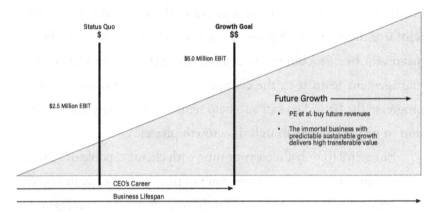

There are lots of pros out there promising to help businesses grow. And when the market hears "grow," it hears "grow profits." But growth drivers are different and lead to a different conversation with clients. Rather than simply promising to help grow profits, growth drivers help their clients understand their growth goals, and—this is critical—they educate their clients about transferable value as the ultimate measure of business success, underscoring that profit does not automatically translate into value, and that as a growth driver, you are uniquely qualified to make the purposeful link between profits and value. Helping the client understand where the engine delivering $2.5 million in profit fits in the normal range of multiples for the industry is important. In terms of transferable value, every dollar of profit can be worth $0.00, $1.00, or perhaps $8.00. It allows us to define ROI in terms of the aspirational multiple. "In addition to growing profits from $2.5 million to $5 million, we will also grow value from the $5 million you could get today to $30 million."

The link between profits and transferable value is not automatic; it needs to be done purposefully. As we will discuss in more depth in the next chapter, the three dimensions of business growth contain three sets of eight objectives and key results (OKRs) (twenty-four in total) that when reached deliver this purposeful link. In the next chapter, we are going to share the methodology and advisory techniques you can use to build a thriving advisory business by delivering killer client results.

Once you feel that you understand the client's growth goal, you can use tools like the three dimensions of growth pyramid to confirm clarity on the information gathered. As you will read in the following chapters, the three dimensions are easy to understand, accelerating the process of highlighting exactly where your client currently sits and what will need to happen to reach the growth goal.

Finally, keep in mind that a CEO's perspective today may not be the same in two or three years because client aspirations change. As the advisor in a long-term growth engagement, you need to check in periodically and confirm the growth goal. Keep in mind that humans are emotional creatures, and as the landscape around us changes, we may change our aspirations as well. Stay in tune with your client.

RECAP

Every engagement needs to start with a deep and detailed growth conversation, a conversation that will also create an important bond between you and the client, a bond of trust.

THE THREE DIMENSIONS
OF BUSINESS GROWTH

After reading this chapter, you will understand the three dimensions of business growth, why these are dimensions and not phases, and the importance of the fourth dimension, time.

Once you understand your client's business goal and their emotional connection to the goal, the next step is to analyze the business that in turn feeds the strategic growth plan design, defined using a series of growth-driving objectives and key results.

We need to think of the business as an engine. Within that engine, the various business processes are the gears, and those gears need to be healthy individually and to intersect with each other inside that engine. For example, if we hire a marketing service to deliver leads, is there an existing sales process to convert the leads? Operational processes to then deliver the new sales? Customer satisfaction intel confirming folks are happy with what they've bought? Financial reporting processes to measure and predict the impact of these new sales? You get the picture. We need a holistic approach. When the gears are not working in sync, businesses lurch from bottleneck to bottleneck.

We want to understand the business's capacity (ability) to predictably generate revenue and profit going into the future. Think about it: when a business operates in a way that delivers predictable profitable cash flow and growth, you have a business that can borrow or raise the capital it can use to scale. You also have a business that is serving its stakeholders. If we can demonstrate a high probability of future revenue and profit—predictability—we also have a valuable business. This chapter is about understanding your client's capacity to grow profits and maximize transferable value using the three dimensions of business growth methodology.

The three dimensions are:

1. Predictable Profits and Cash Flow

2. Predictable Sustainable Growth

3. Predictable Transferable Value

As you are going to see, moving forward in one dimension impacts the other two, allowing you to move your client in all three dimensions simultaneously. Other methodologies tend to mischaracterize the *dimensions* of growth as *phases*, ignoring the fact that any movement within one dimension of a business will affect the other dimensions. *Time*, which can and should be considered the fourth dimension, will be explored later.

LAUNCHING THE ROCKET

Clients want to grow, but you cannot launch a rocket with a slingshot. Ask yourself: Can every business grow? The answer is yes. Every business has the potential to grow if it can harness cash and people to replicable processes. As we learned in chapter 1, 76 percent of CEO clients want to "grow" profits and/or value. The real question then is "How do we launch the growth rocket?" By creating a launchpad. You are the architect of both the launchpad and of the rocket, which you and your client will ride to their "moon," or growth goal. Design and build the launchpad, design and build the rocket, and then light the candle. Here's how.

Would you accept the premise that best-in-class businesses are run using best-in-class processes? If we agree, then reaching the growth goal requires you to identify and work on the operational processes inside your client's business. Which processes meet best-in-class objectives, and which don't? Getting this data helps to define the business's current strategic capacity. You'll need to understand baseline strategic capacity and then prioritize increasing capacity to create a launchpad for growth.

Having strategic capacity means a business has the ability to reach its goals. The goals are usually measured in dollars of revenue and/or dollars of equity value. Its two component parts are growth capacity and value capacity. Growth capacity is a business's ability to predictably deliver sustainable growth. And value capacity is the ability to predictably deliver equity value. Here's what it looks like in a client engagement: your client announces that their goal is to reach $3 million of net income by the end of next year. Great. They currently are at $1.8 million, so it seems like a reach but doable. But ask yourself: Does the business have the people, cash, and processes to get there? That's growth capacity, and as we'll see, this is the realm of Dimensions 1 and 2. Now what if they then say, "And based on the $3 million, we are going to sell the company for $18 million"? Getting there requires value capacity, or the ability to create high confidence in a buyer that the business can continue to grow and deliver cash going into the future. We want our clients to do both in order to have high strategic capacity. Now let's look at the three dimensions.

Our clients rely on us to create *predictable* cash, growth, and transferable value. These are the three dimensions of business growth. Dimensions because the gears in their business engine are intimately interconnected, so this holistic methodology considers every objective and key result within the context of the whole. But we can't work on the whole business; we need to focus on the individual gears. Since there are lots of gears, how do we prioritize them for action? It depends on the goal, right? The three dimensions help professional advisors quickly and efficiently reach their clients' primary strategic goal by correctly prioritizing and strengthening select growth-driving objectives. If a client wants to create predictable cash flow, you aren't going to tell them to get an audit. But if they are preparing to sell, that audit becomes a high priority.

So the first thing after confirming their goal is to gain an understanding of the business from an operational perspective. How does "how" they're running the business compare with the way best-in-class businesses are run? Analyzing the business to establish this baseline allows us to create a strategic growth project plan. The project will leverage existing operational best practices and prioritize the areas that need work. To decide where to focus first, you need the context of the three dimensions of business growth.

All of this helps you communicate the overarching concept that you need every client to grasp: *Immortality*. Businesses with high strategic capacity are what we call immortal. You want to redesign your client's business so that it becomes *immortal*. One of our earliest objectives as an advisor is to help the client understand business immortality. Clients often view their business from the perspective of their own career and fail to create a business that will keep growing even after they have exited. If a business cannot grow without the business owner or CEO, then he or she *is* the business. They are the brains and brawn driving the business forward; they personally create growth capacity. If and when they leave, predictable

> **Businesses with high strategic capacity are what we call immortal.**

cash and growth go with them; therefore, so does value. To create immortality, they need to create high confidence that the business will go on to greater glory without them. The market doesn't reward past performance unless it thinks that this performance is a predictor of future results. At some point, the business will need to have predictable value to a future owner since future performance is the reason they are willing to buy it. Circular but true.

In vetting the three dimensions of business growth and the constituent twenty-four growth-driving objectives, we looked at over a dozen leading resources including:

- Financial audit checklists
- Due diligence checklists
- Quality of earnings checklists
- M&A prep checklists
- Business process engineering best practices
- Business publications
- Private equity discovery processes
- The shoulders of giants through works like *Traction, Scaling Up*, et al.
- and more

These have been distilled, resulting in the growth-drive methodology of objectives and key results that drive growing profits and transferable value.

Pull out your cell phone or laptop and search, "Grow my business." You'll likely be inundated by advertisements for marketing companies, credit card offers, training, all sorts of stuff. Most of it is piecemeal, ad hoc, and certainly *not* addressing the business holistically. While any one of these services might be helpful, they do not provide a complete and full-rounded approach to move the entire business in a given direction.

Let's dispel a myth right here. There is a glamorous but deceiving idea that going to the financial markets and raising outside capital is a common practice. Nope. For most middle-market businesses, this is not a realistic option. Contrast your typical client with a Silicon Valley "entrepreneur" with a venture capital war chest they can use to test and refine products, services, and even the business model itself. Not so for the typical middle-market CEO—they are not handed $50 million to grow a business. Instead, your middle-market client actually has to go and *earn* their working capital, and organic cash is the name of the game.

The next myth commonly believed by middle-market CEOs (let me make a vast generalization here) is that doubling sales will solve all their problems. It can, but it generally does not. Growing a business is extremely expensive. It is like shoveling cash into a furnace. It is even shockingly expensive sometimes. Working capital, calculated by subtracting current liabilities from current assets, directly impacts the speed with which a business can grow. It is vital to remember and communicate to your client that the business can only grow as fast as its free cash flow can fuel it. It stands to reason then that if you're going to grow revenues, you need to start by understanding your client's ability to predictably generate cash flow. Predictable cash flow creates the ability to place low-risk bets on growth. Again, you can't launch a rocket with a slingshot. You need to create a launchpad.

In *Financial Intelligence*, Berman and Knight conclude that the "businesses which are most able to invest in growth are those that can generate their own cash."[17] This quote corroborates Dimension

---

17   Karen Berman and Joe Knight, *Financial Intelligence: A Manager's Guide to Knowing What the Numbers Really Mean* (Boston: HBR Press, 2013).

1. Not only do we want the business to generate its own cash, but we need it to do so predictably. This predictability delivers confidence in forward-looking budgets and thereby in being able to fund the strategic growth project plan for growing profits and value.

Sidebar about how the three dimensions also apply to your advisory business—spoiler alert for chapter 5. High customer satisfaction (Dimension 1 OKR and one of the most important of the twenty-four OKRs) is connected to other growth-driving objectives, driving growth of your advisory business just as it drives the growth of your client's enterprise. Building a thriving advisory business does not depend as much on slick sales and marketing as it does on delivering killer client results. Killer client results lead to high customer satisfaction, and this, in turn, creates repeat clients who become evangelists telling the world how great their experience with you was and arms you for winning strategic referral partners.

Recap: The three dimensions of business growth is an easy-to-explain framework to achieve consistent, predictable profit *and* value growth within a business. The three dimensions of business growth have always existed; focusing on cash, people, and process are not in themselves new ideas. What is new is creating specific actionable Os and KRs, which are prioritized in a proven process for reaching a CEO's goals, be it predictable profit, growth, or transferable equity value.

THE THREE DIMENSIONS OF BUSINESS GROWTH

The three dimensions are defined by three groups of eight growth-driving objectives. Together these describe strategic capacity, divided between growth- and value-driving forces. These objectives guide a business holistically toward predictably growing profits and transferable value. These are dimensions, not phases, and you can move in all three at once. Again, recall the analogy of the business as an engine, with each OKR as a gear; turn one gear and all will move as a result. When you implement a three-dimensional design in your client's business, you create a business that is easier to run, generates sustainable growth, and has maximal transferable value at any given EBITDA (earnings before interest, taxes, depreciation, and amortization). This isn't magic, it's science.

Clients (and unfortunately their uninitiated advisors) often have the cart before the horse. They go merrily about their business assuming that when the day comes to transfer out—to be audited, undergo a quality of earnings analysis or due diligence—that they will be fine. Why wouldn't they be? There is no evidence to the contrary, no warning sign. The business is running smoothly and growing, they pay themselves well … Who wouldn't want to be them? They may view selling the business as simply plugging someone else into their job, with all the benefits that come along with it. Then they decide to sell the business. They meet with an M&A pro and learn that they are like the 95 percent of companies no one would be interested in buying. Their people, cash, and processes do not combine to deliver the strategic capacity needed to survive due diligence.

What is due diligence? Due diligence might be described as a confrontational audit designed to find and quantify risks to future revenues; the typical middle-market business has low strategic capacity, especially in the value capacity area, and therefore presents a poor risk profile. Imagine if this same business got ahold of the due diligence checklist long before they faced the process. What happens to clients who decide to invest the time (best practice is three years) to make sure they can meet all the requirements on the list? Doing so effectively neutralizes risks to future revenue. How then would the meeting with M&A look? Pretty good. If you want to deliver deep value, helping your clients achieve high strategic capacity by implementing Growth-Drive's twenty-four OKRs will have this exact effect.

Breaking it down further: the twenty-four growth-driving objectives together define a best-in-class business. The twenty-four are divided equally among the three dimensions. Each of the eight growth-driving objectives has an average of six key results, which when achieved demonstrate that the business is meeting the objective. We call these OKRs, objectives and key results. Here are the objectives:

	DESCRIPTION	HIGH STRATEGIC CAPACITY OBJECTIVE
1	Effective Senior Leadership	You have an effective leadership team, and the business can run smoothly in your absence.
2	People: Productive and Loyal	Your employees are productive and loyal.
3	High Percentage of Recurring Revenue	You have a high percentage of recurring revenues.
4	Strong Margins	You generate gross and net margins above the industry norm.
5	Financial Reporting Processes	You have strong financial reporting processes.
6	Scalable Sales Process	You use a documented sales process.
7	Strong SOPs	You have documented operational processes.
8	High Customer Satisfaction	You track customer satisfaction.
9	Strategic Vision, Planning, and Execution	You have a written vision, mission, and strategy with the capacity to execute.
10	Strategic Culture	You have a strong culture that you actively nurture.
11	People: Hiring and Training	You can easily hire and train new employees.
12	Large Market Size	The market supports significant growth of your business.

13	Unique Products/Services	Your products and services are unique.
14	Scalable Marketing Process	You use a documented marketing process.
15	Financial: Budget, Forecast, Actuals	You manage the business using a budget.
16	Innovation Creates a Competitive Advantage	You foster innovation in every area of the business.
17	Strategic: Business Story	You have a document a lender or investor could read and get a complete understanding of your business.
18	Financial: Accurate and Credible Financial Reports	Your financial reports and filings are accurate.
19	Legal: IP, Contracts, Governance, and Litigation	Your legal house is in order.
20	High Growth Compared to Market	Your business is growing faster than its competitors.
21	Large Market Share	You have defined your market and niche and have data showing you have dominant market share.
22	Broad Customer Base	Your business generates revenue from a large number of customers.
23	Defensible Market	You can defend your market and future revenues from new competitors.
24	Strong Brand	Your brand is a valuable competitive tool.

There is a bonus twenty-fifth objective, Strength of the M&A Market, which we'll dig into later. Time is the fourth dimension. A holistic strategy must consider the current economic operating environment, and for equity monetization, time to market has a significant impact.

Look at the list carefully and ask yourself: Is this list comprehensive? Are there any glaring omissions? Can this list be applied to more than 80 percent of your clients? Importantly, do you see how achieving the growth-driving objectives creates a business that is aligned with the needs of the shareholders and business owner?

You will also notice that the OKRs split categories that are traditionally lumped together. People is divided into its component parts Senior Leadership, People: Productive and Loyal, and People: Hiring and Training. These are assigned between the launchpad Dimension 1 and the growth Dimension 2. Financial processes are divided between all three dimensions. Why? Because a CEO focused on simply making their business easier to run (a result of reaching Dimension 1 objectives) should prioritize several objectives ahead of hiring new folks (Dimension 2) or making sure they have auditable financials (Dimension 3).

OK, now we need to prioritize the OKRs. The OKRs that are a high priority for creating transferable value may be a low priority for creating predictable cash flow. Let's use an audit as an example. Having several years of audited financials is a best practice for doing an M&A transaction and is therefore accretive to value. But when your client tells you they want to grow cash flow, imagine telling them the first thing they should do is hire an auditor. Irrelevant at this stage, right? It's irrelevant because an audit does little (but not nothing) to create stable cash flow or sustainable growth. It would be better to focus on making their people productive and loyal, having a scalable sales process, maximizing recurring revenues and customer satisfaction, etc.

Let's look at this from the client's perspective. The client has revenue aspirations but is stymied getting there. They sound something like this: "Listen, I just don't understand; I am stuck at $5 million when I should be able to get to $10 million in revenues. We're stuck, and I'm at a loss as to why. Jane down the road did what we're trying to do in just three years. What is she doing that I'm not?" As we will see more clearly in the next chapter, it may be that the CEO himself is the problem. Many middle-market businesses depend heavily on the

CEO to run smoothly. This may feel fine day to day and year to year. Has this CEO ever run a $10 million business? Could it be that the CEO himself hasn't created the strategic capacity to jump his chasm?

Moreover when it comes time to sell the business, due diligence will quickly identify this lack of capacity, leading to a higher discount on price. This is one reason why effective senior leadership is the first objective in Dimension 1. This will be discussed in more detail in the next chapter, but for now, read below to have a better understanding of all three dimensions.

The three dimensions can help you identify and neutralize bottlenecks to growth. Educate your client to operate the business with a rhythm designed to create and maintain momentum, attaining and maintaining the best practices in key areas. This will reduce company-specific risks, and the growth will be managed to minimize chaos and risk.

Side note: Most CEOs assume that doubling profits will double the business's transferable equity value. But they're wrong. In fact, you can double profits and actually *depress* the value of the business. Growth can create chaos; explain this to your client and position yourself as the person who can guide *safe* and *sustainable* growth. The linkage between growth in EBITDA, net income, and shareholder transferable value is not automatic. Rather, this link needs to be fostered, nurtured, and strengthened through documented, replicable, and scalable processes.

Documented replicable processes, leadership delegated with accountability, and a track record of wins all deeply impact the ability to monetize value of the business as well as the multiple at which it monetizes. Explaining the three dimensions of business growth is a great way to show your client where they are today and how to move toward their growth goals.

Always help your clients understand their return on investment from your services in terms of profits *and value*. Once they understand the profit-value equation, you can emphasize your ability to grow the value of a business by two-, six-, or tenfold. This has a proven record of helping the client value your services as an investment rather than a hit to their P&L. By working with you, they are not creating $1 of revenue, they are creating $6 of equity value.

As consultants, even if the CEO's initial energy and desire to begin the process is there, we need to always reinforce their *why*. Have regular check-ins with them on both personal and professional levels: your goal (and it's in your client's best interests) is to maintain the emotional connection to the ultimate goal. With tools and techniques we'll get into later on, you need to keep your finger on the pulse and keep constant vigilance on where they are and where their leadership team is in the execution leadership process. Open discussions plus analysis data shows progress. The hard data can also help reinforce their why and motivation to sustain the business through the growth phases.

> **Only invest your time with clients capable of generating a strong return on their investment of time and treasure in a profit- and value-growth project.**

Pro tip: be careful to only invest your time with clients capable of generating a strong return on their investment of time and treasure in a profit- and value-growth project. You will only know if the client will generate a high return on investment and if this engagement is one in which you can be successful by gaining clarity about what the client needs to do to reach their definition of success. As discussed in the next chapter, clarity can only come from a deep analysis of the client's business.

DIMENSION 1: PREDICTABLE PROFITS AND CASH FLOW

Let's start with Dimension 1: Predictable Profits and Cash Flow. Dimension 1 is the launchpad for growth and the touchstone for all projects. To thrive in Dimension 1, a business must have:

1. Effective Senior Leadership
2. People: Productive and Loyal
3. High Percentage of Recurring Revenue
4. Strong Margins
5. Financial: Use of Financial and Operating Reports
6. Scalable Sales Process
7. Strong SOPs
8. High Customer Satisfaction

Delivering in this dimension creates a business that is easier to run and allows the CEO to reallocate time from day-to-day tasks to long-term strategy. Delivering Dimension 1 moves the needle on strategic capacity, increasing transferable value at current earnings by increasing the multiple at which the business might be sold.

Dimension 1 is the launchpad for growth, creating predictable profits and cash flow. A business that's generating predictable and profitable cash flow is a business that can confidently invest in growth. Why profits *and* cash flow? Because growth is expensive. Cash often gets trapped in the balance sheet, and you need cash *flowing* if you're going to fund growth.

Once you've created this launchpad, you've created three options for your client:

1. *Stay where they are*: You will have helped create a business easier to run with increased value at current EBITA.

2. *Growth*: Your client will be able to *predict* how much cash they have to invest in growth. They will be able to make educated bets on marketing, expanding production facilities, hiring more/better talent, etc.

3. *Monetize value*: The third option you've created is the potential to monetize some or all the value of the business, for example through an M&A transaction. This option is available if the client has high value capacity.

Dimension 1 is also your touchstone. You will periodically reanalyze Dimension 1 OKRs to confirm they remain in line with best practices, maintaining clarity. Dimension 1 needs to stay strong and constantly be reevaluated because its growth-driving objectives are the best-in-class prerequisites for a well-run business.

Dimension 1 lays resilient groundwork that supports the other two dimensions. Differentiating between "profits" and "cash flow" ensures that the business engine is generating adequate free cash flow for growth. There are two threats to free cash flow: cash getting trapped in the balance sheet, and the cash that could fund growth instead going into the owner's pockets. Through focusing on a prioritized plan to expand strategic capacity, you will lead the client to success. With solid progress and a high score in Dimension 1, the business will be primed for predictable profitable growth.

DIMENSION 2: PREDICTABLE PROFITABLE GROWTH

To deliver predictable growth, a business must have:

1. Strategic: Vision, Planning, and Execution

2. Strategic Culture

3. People: Hiring and Training

4. Large Market Size

5. Unique Products/Services

6. Scalable Marketing Process

7. Financial: Budget, Forecasts, Actuals

8. Innovation Creates a Competitive Advantage

As previously mentioned, growth is the number one CEO goal. Most CEOs define growth in terms of increasing profits. Yet remember that the fundamental role of the CEO is to maximize shareholder value in line with the business's vision and strategy. By implementing Dimension 2, Predictable Profitable Growth, the CEO will fulfill their role so long as she or he links the growth of the business to shareholder value. Although not an automatic connection, the methodology described in this book will create and solidify the link.

Moving into Dimension 2 means bringing eight additional growth-driving objectives into the engagement. Think of achieving sustainable growth as analogous to jumping into a swimming pool— you cannot jump into the deep end of the pool without knowing how to swim. Further, once you *can* jump into the deep end, you must *remember* how to swim. That's why you have to establish predictable profits and cash flow first: *This is teaching your client to swim.* As you move toward the deep end, you need to utilize the same *swimming* methodology. You are shifting your focus from stabilizing the business at the shallow end to sustainably growing midpool. The deep end is where value lives.

In the modern ultracompetitive environment of business consulting, practice differentiation against competitors is also key. A given client must see your practice as delivering a maximized return on their investment of time and treasure. The return needs to be communicated both in terms of increased profit as well as in terms of increased value, which is exponential. A dollar of revenue is a dollar, but a dollar of revenue should be four, six, or even ten dollars of transferable value. This means you need to demonstrate the know-how necessary to link growth to transferable equity value. Rather than focusing only on the dollars of new revenue that you've helped them generate, you have taught them that every dollar of revenue could be worth six dollars in wealth.[18]

DIMENSION 3: PREDICTABLE TRANSFERABLE VALUE

To deliver predictable transferable value, a business must have:

1. Strategic: Business Story

2. Financial: History of Accurate and Credible Reports

3. Legal: IP, Contracts, Governance, and Litigation

4. High Growth Compared to Market

5. Large Market Share

6. Diversified Customer Base

7. Defensible Market

8. Strong Brand

Before moving on to Dimension 3, a quick note about the term "value." Business value is described using a number of terms. A formal valuation, as delivered by a CVA, ABV, or ASA, is a regression calculation of the cost of company-specific risk. As you already know, the market rewards risk with discounts, and the valuation more often

---

18   For example, at a 6X multiple, every $1 million of growth is worth $6 million at the deal table. Be the client's hero.

than not is based on discounting cash flow (there are several alternative methodologies) to arrive at a value for the business. Valuations moreover are prepared for a number of non-transfer-related reasons. For example, valuations are calculated for dividing the business asset in divorce, for valuing life insurance, or for reporting to the IRS. These are all very different considerations (and often create different calculations of value) from those impacting a buyer's calculation of price during a transaction.

Ultimately your client is going to be most interested in the value they can convert into wealth, answering, "What's in it for me?" M&A pros use the term "enterprise value" to refer to the value of the business after completing due diligence. Due diligence, which often includes an audit and quality of earnings analysis, is an attempt by the buyer to understand how predictably the business can deliver revenue and profit going into the future. The higher their confidence, the higher the price they'll pay. And the price, you guessed it, is the *transferable* value of the business. Enterprise value and transferable value refer to the same amount. The term "transferable value," which describes the value that a willing buyer would pay for the business after completing due diligence, is descriptive and relatable for clients and is therefore used throughout this book.

Now let's explore Dimension 3, Predictable Transferable Value, because *high transferable value* is the ultimate measure of business success. Want proof? Look at your own investment portfolio and consider the weight you give to the price-to-earnings ratio when making an investment decision. Do you think the typical client will want a high P/E for their business? You bet they do, so let's explore how you'll get them there.

As with the first two dimensions, there are eight growth-driving objectives that round out the strategic capacity that will be scrutinized during M&A due diligence. Due diligence determines price, but contrary to common belief, it does not need to be painful. If you're running a tight ship, due diligence will be an inconvenience, not a catastrophe.

The success rate of mergers and acquisitions (M&A) can vary widely depending on various factors such as industry, size of the companies involved, and the terms of the deal.

Research by *Harvard Business Review* has shown that the failure rate of M&A ranges from 70 percent to 90 percent, meaning that the majority of M&A transactions do not achieve the intended goals. Ultimately the success rate of an M&A transaction depends on many factors, including proper due diligence and clear communication between the parties involved. High strategic capacity communicated through the lens of the three dimensions of business growth improves the due diligence process and promotes clear communication.

There are two main players in due diligence, the buyer and the seller, with diametrically opposed definitions of success. From the seller's perspective, successful due diligence results in a minimum discount on price. Conversely, from the buyer's perspective, successful due diligence will result in the opposite, a maximum discount on price (coupled with a successful transaction). Top-tier clients with high strategic capacity can actually close out due diligence with the buyer offering a premium price. This is due to the ease of transition that you, the advisor, have helped your client establish through documented high strategic capacity.

Now from the buyer's perspective, successful due diligence accurately defines the relative risk a given business presents with regard to future profitable growth. Plenty of high-risk businesses change hands; however, the price paid for these high-risk businesses is low or even liquidation value. Conversely low-risk businesses with high strategic capacity generate much higher prices because the buyer has a greater level of confidence in future profits. Again, let's look back at Dimension 1,which has optimized cash for funding growth by *creating predictable profits and cash flow*. Strength in this dimension is the linchpin of high growth capacity, which when coupled with high value capacity fetches your client the greatest value for their asset at current EBITDA.

So the key to successful due diligence is showing a potential buyer *how* you do what you do, with clearly documented and scalable processes. Dimension 3 cannot stand alone; it requires a history of strength in Dimension 1 and at least a promise of strength in Dimension 2.

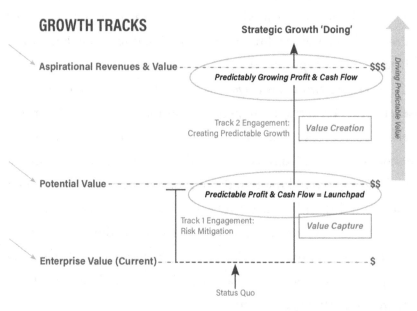

Implementing Dimension 1 typically increases value at current EBITDA. In this chart we see a business that has neutralized company-specific risks to reach its potential value at today's revenues, a.k.a. value *capture*. But what if this value does not deliver the growth goal? You will then need to help the business reach aspirational profits and purposefully link these to value (Dimensions 2 and 3). This is value *creation*. Understanding the difference is key.

THE FOURTH DIMENSION: TIME

Earlier we mentioned time as the fourth dimension. Gauging the amount of time a given client is willing to invest in building strategic capacity is critical to evaluating potential engagement success. Potential outcomes are governed by two time factors: (1) how many years are available to execute a redesign increasing capacity, and (2) where the market will be in the "boom and bust" cycle for an M&A or similar transaction. Unfortunately these are not linked. If it will take three years to maximize value, but the national economy is sliding into recession next year, the road is difficult. During recessions capital seeks quality, fewer transactions are completed, and multiples are conservative. During boom times clients who aren't perfect may successfully complete M&A, and at multiples reflecting a go-go outlook.

If your client has under a year before they want to sell, you're probably in a risk mitigation engagement to maximize value at current revenues. On the other hand, if your client has three or more years, you can meaningfully grow the business profits while simultaneously building value capacity.

Here's an example comparing the results of a one-year and a three-year horizon for the same client engagement. Let's use a straw man trading range for a manufacturing company of 2X–6X EBITDA. Strategic capacity determines the multiple. A manufacturer with low strategic capacity may get a 2X multiple on its $1.7 million of EBITDA, fetching $3.4 million at sale. If this client needs to monetize at $20 million, they will come into the engagement assuming they'll need to increase revenues to $10 million if they hope to hit their number. Here is where time has a profound impact:

- *One-Year Window*: All focus is on mitigating risk and moving their multiple from 2X to 6X. The best-case scenario is a transferable value of $10.2 million.

- *Three-Year Window*: Armed with clarity about linking revenues to transferable value, you can confidently educate your client that by only *doubling* revenues, along with increasing strategic capacity, they can drive value almost 600 percent to and reach their aspirational goal of $20 million. A great way to explain this is by comparing your skills to doing a self-directed private equity play.

Time to execute has a deep and lasting impact on the business, the type of buyer the client business can attract, and the end result for the business owners, employees, stakeholders, and community.

Time to market is also a critical factor. The strength of the buyer market is an external value driver that cannot be controlled, but we can always choose *when* to sell. Let's use a real-world example of the owner of an equipment supply business in South Carolina. The national economy, and therefore the M&A market follows roughly ten-year cycles. In the first quarter of 2022, the market is white hot and is going to stay positive through 2023 or even 2024 depending on macroeconomic conditions. For planning purposes, the advisor's research indicates that after 2024 the market will likely soften, becoming a buyer's market. The next strong seller's market will be in the early 2030s. After this discussion the owner understood the impact on price and their career of staying the course and took action to build wealth through ongoing operation of the business for the next decade.

If your client isn't willing to stay in their business for ten years, you need to educate them about the trade-off they are making between selling now and selling later. The strategic plan you create needs to account for where the market is, the time your client wants to take to move toward selling, and where the market is likely to be at that point. This can be as simple as a footnote. Also recall the transformational mindset described in chapter 1 and create contingency plans for deviations in the expected market schedule.

PUTTING IT TOGETHER: ENGAGEMENT TIMELINE AND CLIENT ROI

Your typical middle-market business owner or CEO has misconceptions about the best method of growth for their business. When you ask, "What's the biggest problem facing your business?" you may hear back, "I don't have enough leads ... I don't have enough customers... I don't have enough revenue." Based on this misunderstanding of the problem, clients blindly chase leads and customers, thinking this will solve all their woes. But solving the wrong problem can burn cash while creating drama and chaos. Sometimes they'll succeed in growing top-line revenues and see profit *decrease* because robust growth can drive cash flow into the cellar.

Engagement Timeline: Three Dimensions of Business Growth
Increasing client cash flow and value by applying the growth-drive action cycle, leading clients as they create predictable profits, growth, and transferable value.

	Predictable Profits and Cash Flow *Launchpad for Growth*	Predictable Growth *#1 CEO Goal*	Predictable Transferable Value *Ultimate Measure of Success*
Growth-Driving Objectives	1. Effective **Senior Leadership** 2. **People:** Productive and Loyal 3. High Percentage of **Recurring Revenue** 4. Strong **Margins** 5. Fin: Use of **Financial and Operating Reports** 6. Scaleable **Sales Process** 7. Strong **SOP** 8. High **Customer Satisfaction**	1. **Strategic:** Vision, Planning, and Execution 2. **People:** Strategic Culture 3. **People:** Hiring and Training 4. Large **Market Size** 5. Unique **Products/Services** 6. Scaleable **Marketing Process** 7. **Fin:** Budget and Forecasting 8. **Innovation**	1. **Strategic:** Business Story 2. **Fin:** History of Accurate and Credible Reports 3. **Legal:** IP, Contracts, Governance, and Litigation 4. High **Growth** Compared to Market 5. Large **Market Share** 6. Diversified **Customer Base** 7. Defensible **Market** 8. Strong **Brand**

By educating your client that trying to increase revenues without increasing growth capacity *will not* fix their problems, you connect your expertise to their goals. They will soon understand that the better plan is to bring the business in line with Dimension 1 OKRs at current revenues *and then* work on Dimension 2 and growing revenue.

Here is a case that illustrates, in the CEO's words:

"We grew exponentially year after year after year, doubling the size of the business every year. It created absolute production chaos, and although we were profitable on paper, all of our profits were tied up in inventory and production. And at the end of the day, we were starved for cash, even with a significant cash infusion from a professional investor. We ultimately couldn't break through that cash crunch because of the impact of the great recession of 2008. In the go-go time from 2003–2007 orders accelerated exponentially, while our production capacity had a linear increase. In 2009–2010 orders dropped off the cliff, cutting off our major source of working capital, which forced us to cut production and eventually close our doors. I would have told you in 2007 that doubling sales would solve all of our problems; in fact it was killing us. We didn't know what we didn't know, so we kept doing the wrong things trying to make things right. Turns out growing killed us."

If the client had understood and focused on the powerful Dimension 1 OKRs, they may have had the knowledge needed to save the business.

THE THREE DIMENSIONS AND A GROWTH-DRIVING ACTION CYCLE

As we discussed in the introduction, a growth-driving action cycle is analyze, design, and execute, repeated in turn. Analysis allows you to gain total clarity about what clients need to get to where they want to go. Design converts the clarity into prioritized objectives and key results. Next, execution sprints deliver increasing strategic capacity. You then return to analysis to discover whether reaching one objective, like increasing sales, is creating a bottleneck elsewhere, for example in delivery and customer satisfaction.

Execution does not explicitly exist within the growth-driving objectives. This is why you must spend time during discovery understanding if the client has an execution leadership system. The execution leadership system prevents blockages in deploying the strategic plan. Effectively using an execution leadership system means using data to confirm the proper prioritization of growth-driving objectives, which dictate the rhythm of sprints to meet OKRs. Without execution embedded early in the process, the plan will remain just that, a plan. Execution moves that plan into reality.

Remember: The client does not necessarily need to be operating at best practice for all the growth-driving objectives in order to create positive change. Creating high strategic capacity across the totality of the client's operations in a short period of time is impossible. And perfection itself is impossible. There is no such thing as a perfect business. To move from status quo to the growth goal requires prioritizing

> **There is no such thing as a perfect business.**

objectives and checking boxes next to their key results. Doing this on a sustained basis and building objective upon objective drives predictable profits, sustainable growth, and a gradual maximization of transferable value. This is accomplished through the execution leadership system described in chapter 10.

A note about transparency. Execution depends on people. Execution also creates friction. How do we promote engagement and drive execution with minimized friction? The best tool for driving successful execution is transparency. Transparency helps foster a transformational mindset with the leaders and employees who are charged with delivering results. People naturally resist change because they fear the unknown. Transparency about mission, strategy, goals, and success metrics shines a bright light on the future, mitigating resistance. Transparency allows people to *manifest* change within the business. Transparency also has a proven track record of increasing employee engagement (People: Productive and Loyal), creating the full buy-in from employees and the executive team. This ensures your engagement will not fall flat over time as it unavoidably creates friction. Transparency can be created by keeping score using tools like flash reports, which we cover in chapter 9.

One more note: An execution leadership system deployed across the entire organization is a key contributor to a strategic culture. When transparency and the transformational mindset is embedded into the business culture as a whole, it acts as oil to lubricate the gears of the business engine, avoiding friction as we guide the client upward.

So we have analyzed the business and identified the growth-driving objectives on which to work to create high Dimension 1 capacity. We then move into Dimension 2, pouring leads into the sales process, and sales is doing their job to generate new revenues and net new orders that need to be delivered. The strong SOPs from Dimension 1 must be resilient enough to keep up with Dimension 2's net new sales, and the processes, procedures, and track record of success are laying the groundwork for Dimension 3.

You must anticipate the potential negative impact that net new orders can have on operational delivery. By winning in one area, we might be creating chaos in another. Always analyze, design, and execute and circle back, asking, "Are we still strong in these core, touchstone areas? Can we continue with our growth plan? Or is there anything on which we need to work before we move forward?"

It's a key differentiator for us as advisors that the three dimensions of business growth is a strategic capacity-driving methodology. We are always looking at the whole of the business. Subject matter consultants tend to bring the same hammer and nail to solve a single problem under the guise of helping the entire business, and all too often create chaos. Growth advisors who focus on strategic capacity solve issues on a system-wide basis, avoiding chaos. By talking openly about this difference, you ensure that the CEO won't pigeonhole you as a CPA or a management consultant or a human resources pro. They'll understand you as a business advisor who can lead them by applying a methodology that considers the entire business both within its own context and against the market. This positions you as a peer with the CEO who can help them increase growth capacity and value capacity and deliver their win.

Remember that a CEO's perspective today may not be the same in two or three years' time because client aspirations change. As the advisor in a long-term growth engagement, you need to check in periodically and confirm the growth goal and maintain emotional fuel. Keep in mind that humans are emotional creatures, and as the landscape around us changes, we may change our aspirations as well. Stay in tune with your client.

RECAP

Let's recap the chapter and use it to shed light on a couple of other points. Remember, the three dimensions of business growth is a holistic methodology. You can implement Dimension 1 on its own and create a happy client. This in turn can also be the launchpad for growth and for creating predictable transferable value, getting a handle on controlling what the value of the business will be. When you apply the three dimensions to strategic plan design, you're going to deliver on all three of the dominant CEO goals: make the business easier to run, grow the business, and obtain high transferable value.

Let's stress again: Dimension 1 is the launchpad for growth, and it's the touchstone for all the dimensions. We are always going to look back at Dimension 1 to make sure the business maintains best-in-class performance in these eight OKRs. The three dimensions link growth to transferable value, and you can move a client in all three dimensions at the same time. The three dimensions have twenty-four OKRs, with eight prioritized OKRs for each dimension detailed in chapters 5, 6, and 7. Reaching the client's win, their growth goal is a matter of increasing strategic capacity through well-understood and proven actionable steps. Private equity groups do this day in and day out, and by deploying the three dimensions and increasing strategic capacity, you are helping your client do a self-directed private equity play that moves their business where they want it to go while creating wealth for the owner and their stakeholders. This is how you deliver killer results.

CONDUCTING DEEP ANALYSIS

After reading this chapter, you will understand the importance of conducting deep analysis on your client's business operations and the tools that will help you create total clarity about what your client needs to get the success they want.

As discussed in the introduction and briefly repeated in the previous chapter, the growth-drive action cycle is analyze, design, and execute. In this chapter, we are going to discuss how to conduct a deep analysis of your client's business, during which you are creating absolute clarity about what's going on in the business. With this clarity you can make informed decisions about redesigning the business so that it can deliver your client's goal, whether it be growth, operational freedom, or transferable value. You can use an analog tool like questionnaires or a pre–due diligence checklist or a more sophisticated technology-based tool like the CLARITY Strategic Capacity Analysis. But before devising a plan, you must be fully in touch with the current state of the business. There are a lot of different ways to perform this analysis, but all routes lead to about the same place: a mountain of data. An understanding of this data in turn helps you create a plan to redesign the business from its status quo to a humming profit-and-value-delivering engine.

A *healthy* business generates outputs predictably. It generates those outputs based on a well-understood set of processes. The outputs—revenue and profit—can be discussed in terms of generally accepted accounting principles (GAAP). Why is GAAP important? When we say profits, we all know what that means because the term "profit" is defined in GAAP. Similarly when we say net income, we all know what that means. GAAP serves as a lingua franca within business when discussing financial figures.

> **A *healthy* business generates outputs predictably. It generates those outputs based on a well-understood set of processes.**

Thanks to GAAP, there is a common understanding of defined financial terms, allowing us to compare financial performance between businesses by comparing apples to apples. Analogous to this would be a common understanding of the best practices around business operations. When you educate your client and their senior leadership team about the best practices for running critical business processes, you are leading them to a common understanding of their goals and accountabilities. Deep analysis creates total clarity about a business's strategic capacity to deliver sustainable growth while maximizing transferable value, enabling transparency, and promoting communication.

Your analysis should discover how well your client's business processes line up against best-in-class operations. Operating in line with best practices drives growth, and your job is to create this process alignment and improve the business. You may ask, "Why are best practices the critical yardstick against which you must measure your client?" Because best practices provide context for performance: You're either operating in line with the best and brightest within your industry, or you're not. And you guessed it, businesses operating according to best practices have high strategic capacity delivering robust growth and high transferable value.

Analysis generates the data that powers strategy. Deep analysis creates total clarity about a business's strategic capacity to deliver sustainable growth while maximizing transferable value. Businesses with high strategic capacity are most likely to outperform their peers. To make capacity actionable, deep analysis should create a strategic capacity score. This score, as we will see in a case study later in this chapter, predicts how well the business can currently drive sustainable growth in both cash flow and transferable value, the twin measures of business success.

Strategic capacity considers performance in all three dimensions of business growth. However, as a concept strategic capacity is not focused enough for the purpose of leading clients toward their goals. To sharpen focus, strategic capacity should properly be divided into its two constituent aspects: growth capacity and value capacity. A business with high growth capacity and high value capacity has high strategic capacity. Growth capacity refers to the business's current ability to deliver sustainable growth compared to best-in-class operations. This considers the people, cash, and processes of Dimensions 1 and 2. Value capacity refers to the business's current ability to monetize transferable value. This predicts their ability to successfully complete the normal due diligence required to successfully complete an M&A or similar transaction, considering all three dimensions and weighted for Dimension 3.

To illustrate this principle, let's use the following table where growth capacity is the x-axis, and value capacity is the y-axis. Low strategic capacity is in the lower left, and high strategic capacity is in the upper right. A business with high strategic capacity can predictably deliver growth while also presenting a low-risk profile and therefore high transferable value.

By measuring strategic capacity in the x- and y-axes, you educate your client, creating clarity and dispelling voodoo. "Voodoo" is what we call that soup of assumptions, chasing shiny objects, bad habits, and complacency seen so often in middle-market businesses. You either have clarity or are ruled by voodoo. In addition, understanding strategic capacity answers two questions for the business owner: (1) Why would someone buy this business? and (2) Why wouldn't they?

Here's how the clarity created by deep analysis plays out. The business in this case is in manufacturing NAICS thirty-one to thirty-three with annual EBITDA of $3.5 million. The range of multiples (rounded) is 3X–6X EBITDA. The business has a strategic capacity score of fifty-nine of one hundred, at the high end of typical middle-market businesses when they first engage an advisor. The component growth capacity score is also fifty-nine, and the value capacity score is forty-eight.

The results reflect the real world: A business in the lower left zone presents as not able to deliver predictable sustainable growth, nor does it have the attributes required for transferring value like a defensible market, audited financials, etc. The result? No sale/liquidation value. A business in the upper right zone has high growth capacity and high value capacity, therefore robust and predictable growth. It creates confidence that this growth will continue going into the future and has its financial and legal houses in order. The same EBITDA will deliver vastly different transferable values. Ask yourself: Which business would you buy—upper right or something else? And if something else, what would you pay for it?

Value at Low Multiple	Value at High Multiple
$10,430,000	$21,035,000

IMPACT OF CAPACITY ON TRANSFERABLE VALUE

	Low Growth Capacity	Moderate Growth Capacity	High Growth Capacity
High Growth Capacity Score > 85	$3,129,000	$12,586,000	$21,035,000
Moderate Growth Capacity	$1,564,500	$10,517,500	$15,732,500
Low Growth Capacity	$0.00	$6,258,000	$10,430,000

score < 40

Low Growth Capacity	Moderate Growth Capacity	High Growth Capacity Score > 85

The highlighted value in the center grid provides guidance as to likely transferable value at current strategic capacity.

It won't surprise you to learn that best-in-class businesses have well-defined objectives for growing revenues—and an additional set of objectives for creating high transferable value. Reaching these objectives produces scalability and predictability. Here's an example: If the best practice for margins is to produce gross and net margin above the industry norm, then this is the definition of success. Your client is either above, at, or below this objective. As we dig in, you'll learn the ripple effect reaching each objective can have on every other aspect of the business. If a business is an engine, the output of which is revenue and profit, then best practices are the gears in this engine. Gears because they all work together to deliver results. Every business should produce revenue in a proven and systematic way, ensuring the business is sustainable and not simply based on the efforts of certain individuals.

We described the gears as growth-driving objectives in earlier chapters. In turn, when you measure your client against these best practices, you discover how to help them improve. The secret is in measuring all the gears before doing any work. Like the deep discovery accomplished with the growth conversation, you must complete a deep discovery about all the gears in the business engine if we are to understand the engine as a whole. Understanding the business as a whole creates total clarity about what our client needs to get the success they want. This clarity about the predictable performance of the business also allows us to improve weak gears and monitor strong gears. In simple terms, deeply understanding the business allows for holistically redesigning the business so that it becomes an efficient vehicle that can confidently deliver the growth goal.

Analyzing the whole business engine accomplishes another goal: It differentiates you from your competitors (a Dimension 2 Predictable Growth best practice). Clients can pigeonhole advisors based on misconceptions. If you are an accountant, they may assume that you will only focus on finances. If you are a valuator, they may think you should be talking about value. They may question why a management consultant is asking about financial reporting processes. By leading your client through a detailed analysis of the totality of their operations, including strategic and tactical forces, you show yourself as a peer to the CEO, as a senior professional who is a specialist at understanding the business holistically, and therefore as the right person to help the business thrive.

> **Deeply understanding the business allows for holistically redesigning the business so that it becomes an efficient vehicle that can confidently deliver the growth goal.**

Total clarity also helps us to evolve from the bad habit of looking at business results and implying an understanding of the related processes. That habit is akin to looking at how fast an athlete completes the four-hundred-yard dash and implying their height, weight, and physical health, metabolic performance, recovery times, history of injuries, etc. In both cases we cannot know for sure without additional data. By running a holistic analysis of the business, you're taking a look into reality rather than implying an understanding of reality by interpreting the results. Analyzing the business in terms of clear inter-related processes of gears allows the client to reorient themselves as the dynamics of the gears within the business engine change.

Let's consider private equity (PE) as a community of successful growth drivers. PE has an enviable track record of buying and growing the revenues and value of middle-market businesses. Ask yourself: How does PE decide what companies to buy? What to pay for these companies (transferable value)? How to grow these companies in a replicable and predictable fashion? It's not magic, it's process, and the process starts with analyzing where a business is compared to best practices. PE uses due diligence and other means. So do all professional investors. Shouldn't you?

We know that best-in-class businesses use best-in-class operational practices. Now let's add the next layer: If we consider best practices as our objectives, what tells us that we are making progress toward them? The answer is to divide each objective into measurable constituent parts, referred to here as key results. These are operational and process results, not financial results. The key results are stepping stones in implementing best practices. Together, these are objectives and key results (OKRs[19]) and are the building blocks for increasing strategic capacity, enabling growing profits and transferable value.

Let's look briefly at Os and KRs before discussing what a deep analysis looks like. Objectives define the thing that needs to be

---

19   See *Measure What Matters: How Google, Bono, and the Gates Foundation Rock the World with OKRs* by John Doerr.

achieved. They are quarterly, measurable, and qualitative. They can be connected or downsized so the senior leadership team or individual team members can link and coordinate their objectives with those of the CEO or shareholders. Objectives tell you where you want to be. In turn, key results are the steps that have to be taken in order to achieve the objective they help deliver. Keep in mind that objectives and goals are not the same thing—objectives help deliver goals. Like objectives, the key results have to be measurable, quantifiable, and time bound.

Here's an example using the best practice objective for senior leadership:

Objective: Your business has an effective leadership team that is aligned with and accountable to the business's vision and mission, helping the shareholders achieve their objectives.

- Key Result 1: The shareholders have defined time-bound objectives for the business.

- Key Result 2: The senior leadership team understands and aligns with the business's vision, mission, and strategy.

- Key Result 3: Senior leadership is accountable to the business's vision, mission, and strategy.

- Key Result 4: The business runs smoothly in the senior leader's absence.

- Key Result 5: The business has a succession plan for each senior leader.

Add a date after each of these and suddenly you have a plan. Do the things needed to make the key result true by the specified date and you have execution.

When you have the initial meeting with the client, you might ask whether they have an effective senior leadership team and how the business runs when the CEO is not there. How long can the CEO be gone from the business before it becomes a problem? This should be conversational and not challenging. But what you really want to know is whether there is an effective senior leadership team aligned with and accountable to the business's vision and mission, helping the shareholders achieve their goals. While this is not something to be asked during the initial conversation, it is essential for deep analysis.

All the analysis will feed a redesign of your client's business so that it will align with the best practices defined in the three dimensions of business growth, teaching your client how to manage the business guided by objectives and monitored through key results. Objectives become the stepping stones of strategic execution. And when you assign a key result to an individual and apply a due date, you create individual accountability. Add it to the flash report and you have transparency that promotes team accountability and collaboration. In short, a business delivering key results, building to objectives, and confidently moving toward its goals is running like a best-in-class operation.

Key results are implemented in steps called sprints (see chapter 8). The execution of sprints is accomplished with a plan that builds strength upon strength, while always keeping holistic vigilance on the business engine. Building strength is good, but of course the law of unintended consequences applies, which is precisely why you should use an analyze-design-execute cycle. Here's an example:

1. Your client has strong SOPs: The business has strong, documented standard operating processes that ensure consistent successful delivery on the promises made to the marketplace by sales. You've scored the growth-driving objective at the outset of your engagement, therefore at current load. So far so good.

2. Next, your client implements a scalable sales process, and sales begin to hum, with orders coming in at higher-than-ever volumes.

3. As your engagement moves into Dimension 2, the team creates a scalable marketing process, and higher-quality leads are passed on to sales. Sales volume increases yet again.

4. Circling back to operations, this newfound sales volume is threatening to overwhelm production capacity, hurting recurring revenue, customer satisfaction, people: effective and loyal (morale), and the brand.

We touch on sprints here to underscore the holistic impact that your work has on the business and the need to keep in close touch with your client and their OKRs.

Breaking objectives down into time-bound key results puts the entire project on a timescale that flows dynamically. Wise advisors use weekly check-ins, which are necessary to keep any client on track. You will keep your finger on the pulse and help the business execute the analyze-design-execute cycle over the long term. One way is to think of the progression between the various OKRs as a relay race. When a key result is achieved, you start the next, and then the next, and you steadily move toward the finish line.

There are a couple of ways to set time constraints on key results. You can plan backward from a desired delivery date. If your client says, "I want to sell my business within the year," you can start planning backward from the requirements for a successful transaction. You can also plan forward based on the time it takes to reach each key result. By waterfalling objectives, you implement growth-driving objectives from day one and therefore have a rough prediction of the time required to reach the ultimate profit and/or equity value goal.

Typically clients have some level of existing analysis and reporting. Most of the ways in which we normally talk about business are finance-based; there are dollar signs attached, as would be found in a budget. And yet most clients have low control over their numbers. How many of your clients can understand and explain their balance sheet? How many generate timely and accurate P&L and cash flow reports? And do they know how to interpret their P&L and balance sheet? Before controlling their numbers, they must understand them. The OKRs therefore focus significantly on how your client gathers financial and other metrics and how they use this information to manage the business. This means you need to analyze the business to discover both information gathering and information use. Analyze-design-execute is a cycle. You must make sure that you are routinely (at least quarterly) going back and analyzing the business, identifying if new growth-based stresses have been put on the engine that need to be addressed.

Putting it all together, let's address how you use your analysis to inform your engagements. There are three models: 1) Analyze the business with the CEO and then confirm the analysis with the senior leadership team; 2) complete the analysis with the senior leaders and present your findings to the CEO; or 3) run the analysis with the CEO and their senior team together. Deciding which path to take is driven by the case, and one of your jobs is to suss out the best path. Although adding more voices to the conversation can be a bit chaotic, only the leadership team together can provide an accurate analysis and total clarity on the business. Analyzing the business with a group may take more time, but it also delivers a consensus view of where the business truly is.

Before we look more in depth at just one of the growth-driving objectives from Dimension 1, a word about tying roles to process.

Since growth-driving objectives and key results are the keys to success, they can be referenced when writing senior leadership (and employee) job descriptions. These descriptions need to be connected to the vision, mission, and strategy of the business. The data tells us that 22 percent of companies do not have a strategic plan. No plan, no OKRs, therefore no direct, written connections between roles and accountability; this becomes a top growth killer and deal killer.

Defining roles can immediately connect the business process to accountability. For instance, the Dimension 1 OKR People: Productive and Loyal, is defined as "every employee and contractor understands their role and the metrics defining their success, both from an individual perspective and tied to the team contributing to the goals of the business." If we're writing a description for the VP of Sales, we could say that they are accountable to the president for preparing and executing the sales plan and repeatable sales process to deliver on revenue goals. This description is pulled straight from the scalable sales process OKR. If defining a team, we might say that "the delivery team is accountable to the VP of Operations for successfully executing the delivery process and meeting delivery objectives; success means delivering X units per day, each of which meets or exceeds minimum quality metrics." Do you see how efficient tying roles to OKRs is? And it lays the groundwork for the execution leadership system.

WORKING TOGETHER PULLING THE OARS: THE IMPORTANCE OF SENIOR TEAM ALIGNMENT

Senior leadership plays a strategic role. Strategy is the plan for moving forward to the business's vision. It stands to reason then that an effective senior leadership team should be aligned as to the vision, mission, and strategy, as they also must be aligned on the accuracy of the business analysis of strategic capacity. If the senior team is not aligned, then they are not all on the same starting line or using the same map when the work begins to reach the growth goal. A deeply impactful first project is therefore to confirm senior leadership's alignment with the defined goal, the strategy for reaching it, and the business's current strategic capacity.

This can be a delicate process because you are treading a potential minefield and realigning ingrained bad habits, animosities, rivalries, internal politics, low commitment, and more. Like the original growth conversation, it needs to play out, not be jammed into an artificial time box. If necessary, you'll use two or three half-day sessions to lead a discussion that creates total clarity and consensus. While there is training available to develop the moderating skills you need to more effectively lead this conversation, you can use the OKRs as your meeting agenda, put each growth-driving objective on the board, and lead a group discussion about how the business stacks up. Be the guide on the side as the team debates business performance. What you will see next is magic.

You are there as a facilitator of this deep-dive workshop. You, the advisor, must challenge them to be concrete and honest, and you should not be surprised when each senior leader views performance differently. There's a discussion point here: Why are perspectives different? By listening you'll discover there are times where some members of the leadership team do not necessarily understand an objective. Sometimes you may need to explain and give meaning to some of the important growth-driving objectives, as every senior leader may not be in touch with the operations of other areas of the business. You're getting at the truth and almost guiding them, without giving them the truth yourself. Trust the process; they will come to the right conclusion.

A note about senior leadership teams. There's a difference between management and leadership. High-performing businesses have senior leadership teams, in contrast to ho-hum businesses run by managers. Now managers can get along, can be friends, can be what we call "collegial." Collegial teams are nice. But collaborative teams are better—and they need not be friends. From talking with hundreds of advisors, senior leadership teams often think they are collaborative, but they are in fact only collegial. What's the difference? Collegial teams get along, but collaborative teams look beyond niceties and push each other to perform. Collaboration is far more than simply getting along. In fact, getting along is not a must-have. A senior team has to be able to constructively criticize each other, so try to foster this mindset. Ask them up front to give you permission to challenge the room, creating a safe space for constructive criticism to lead to newfound clarity in roles and responsibilities and unity of mission. In situations where this environment has not been created, the conversation can get heated quickly, sometimes even in terms of pushback against you, so do your best to buffer the blow by fostering that transformational mindset we discussed earlier.[20]

Ideally, in a collaborative environment you are able to spin several gears at once. The following examples provide a framework for understanding how this should work:

1. High Percentage of Recurring Revenues: collaboration among sales, operations, financial, and legal.

2. Financial Report and Operating Reports: collaboration among senior leadership, sales, operations, and finance.

3. High Customer Satisfaction: collaboration among operations, human resources, and sales.

---

20 Patrick Lencioni's *The Five Dysfunctions of a Team* is a terrific resource for digging deeper into this topic.

4. Strong Brand: Brand is the outward manifestation of strategic culture and therefore depends on strong collaboration among leaders charged with customer satisfaction, operations, marketing, human resources, and product differentiation.

5. Defensible Market: Collaboration among legal, finance, operations, and product differentiation will create and maintain barriers.

When it comes to the issue of the CEO being in the room for the deep analysis, it's a judgment call that requires some understanding of the dynamics of the senior leadership team and the personality of the CEO. In most cases we would prefer to have the CEO present, but before they enter, he or she should be ready for the conversation to be a learning exercise. Emphasize that he or she will be able to express themselves later, but first they must listen, bite their tongue, and thank the staff for the feedback. Remember, there is no good news or bad news, only data. This is an important part of leadership. If the CEO is unable to be in the room, then that should tell you an awful lot about the senior team, the leadership style, and the culture in the organization—none of it being good.

A CASE STUDY: RIDGE SPECIALTY TOOLING

Let's look at the following case study to more completely understand what a deep analysis of a business looks like only in relation to senior leadership and how a problem in one gear of the business engine can impact others. Ridge is owned and run by Diane, who worked with Steve, a veteran growth advisor.[21] Let's look at how the deep analysis of Ridge's capacity was leveraged to increase Steve's ability to drive the client forward.

---

21 All names are fictional and key facts have been blurred to protect privacy.

Before the engagement even started, Steve led Diane through the growth conversation. Steve used sophisticated discovery techniques to help Diane define her dreams for herself, her family, and the business and to gain clarity on the business's capacity to deliver these dreams. Remember that the very act of discussing Ridge's capacity in the context of defined best practices helped Diane decide to get the ball rolling. When it comes to motivating a team, there is no substitute for the psychological impact of the senior leaders hearing themselves say that the way they are operating does not meet the best-in-class bar. The trust and value from this discussion led Diane to hire Steve, whose first project used deep analysis of the business to help Diane understand Ridge Specialty Tooling's strengths and bottlenecks.

We need to understand a business in the context of best practices, a.k.a. strategic capacity, so a score is crucial. If high strategic capacity is one hundred, where does Diane fall? Deep analysis of Ridge delivered a growth capacity score of 56 percent and value capacity score of 47 percent (these scores are discussed in more detail elsewhere). The process showed Diane that without executing a redesign of her business, she could not reach her personal and professional goals (dreams). This had the additional effect of creating that emotional link between Steve's expertise, fixing the business, and Diane's personal wealth. Deep analysis also identified deal killers that would need to be cleared before attempting to monetize value through an M&A or other transaction.

We'll focus on effective senior leadership to illustrate the impact of deep analysis. But before we do, let's recap a few business fundamentals. Here is why businesses exist and what roles Diane should be playing:

- Businesses exist to deliver a return to the shareholders. This is as true for private companies as it is for those that are publicly traded.

- Ideally the shareholders are represented by a board of directors. The board sets profit and transferable value business goals.

- The fundamental role of the CEO is to meet these shareholder goals and maximize shareholder value within the guidelines of the mission and vision.

- The CEO is therefore accountable to the board and through the board to the shareholders.

- The CEO's job is to delegate authority, with accountability to the shareholders' goals, through the senior leadership team up into the entire organization.

Now we can all agree that for a middle-market CEO like Diane, this gets fuzzy. She is the only shareholder, has no board, does not understand her fundamental role (or more precisely has lost track of it in the day-to-day operations of the business), and has built the systems and culture on the cornerstone of her control. This is a great example of middle-market businesses who as a group present with severely limited growth and value capacities.

Hopefully you are now getting a sense of why having an effective senior leadership team is the first growth-driving objective in Dimension 1. Here is the effective leadership team in OKR detail:

Objective: Your business has an effective leadership team that is aligned with and accountable to the business's vision and mission, helping the shareholders achieve their objectives.

Key results, which guide bringing the business in line with this growth-driving objective, with emphasis added:

1. The shareholders have written time-bound goals for the business that are shared with the senior leadership team.
   - *Diane's answer: "Partly true."*

2. The senior leadership team understands and is aligned with the shareholder goals.

    ▫ *Diane's answer: "No."*

3. Senior leadership is accountable to the shareholder goals.

    ▫ *Diane's answer: "Not really." Logical since she had not shared the goal with her team.*

4. Senior leadership meets regularly to review and discuss progress toward the shareholder goals.

    ▫ *Diane's answer: "No."*

5. The business runs smoothly in the CEO's absence.

    ▫ *Diane's answer: "Partly true." Like many middle-market business owners and CEOs, Diane maintained tight control on information and decision making, and the true answer was "Not really."*

6. The business has a succession plan for each senior leader.

    ▫ *Diane's answer: "Not really."*

By the way, "The business runs smoothly in the CEO's absence" is present in some form on every due diligence checklist. Bet on it coming up in the first meeting with a prospective acquirer. Your role as the growth advisor before this question is asked is to make sure the answer will be a resounding "Yes."

Let's game out the impact of deep analysis on just this one objective through Diane and Steve's experience with Ridge.

During the growth conversation, Diane and Steve discovered that she had an $18 million equity value gap: they would need to gross $18 million from the sale of the business in order to supplement existing assets and fully fund her target lifestyle. At present, after satisfying transaction costs, debt, taxes, and other shareholders, Diane would only gross $2.1 million even in a best-case scenario at Ridge's current strategic capacity. During the conversation Diane set her sights on five years to close this wealth gap. She learned from working with Steve that she would need to lead her team and business to increase margin to 10 percent, while increasing growth and value capacities. Much of the win would come from increasing the multiple Ridge could get in an M&A transaction. The business goal was defined as Plan Year Five revenue of $33 million with net income of $3.3 million.

During an initial summary analysis, Diane indicated that it was partly true that the business ran smoothly in her absence. A more sophisticated deep analysis revealed that "partly true" was a fairy tale. In reality the business needed her every day, a common plight of middle-market CEOs. The problem with such a situation is that the "Do-It-All" CEO is the number one growth killer and number one deal killer.

Deep analysis expanded Diane's and Steve's understanding. The analysis identified that what she had not done was establish a time-bound value goal nor had she shared her "big" goals with the senior leadership team. Why? Diane was worried about the team's reaction to learning that the business might be sold one day.

Steve also ran an abbreviated analysis with the whole senior team, asking one question about each of the twenty-four growth-driving objectives so that he (and Diane) could get a grip on the team's view of strategic capacity. Here are their answers. CEO Diane is respondent three.

Effective Senior Leadership	You have an effective leadership team, and the business can run smoothly in your absence.
The business runs smoothly in my absence	
Partly true	1, 3
Not really	
No	2, 4, 5

No one, including Diane, thought the business could run smoothly in her absence. Besides Diane, only one other member of the team thought it was partly true, and three (or 60 percent) answered with a flat "No." If the team is to be accountable for helping Diane reach her goals, they need to share accountability for running the business. And if they are to be accountable to this objective, we need to define what "the business running smoothly" means, right?

The analysis process itself educated Diane on the standards to which professionals like private equity groups hold their portfolio businesses. Diane saw that she and her team could either implement best practices or leave money on the M&A deal table. Powerful motivation. And if value is the goal, it might make sense to share some of the value with the team, increasing their Productive and Loyal quotient. Like gears in the engine.

Once Diane understood the importance of creating an effective senior leadership team, Steve helped her create and execute a sprint (project) to up their game. Using the data from Ridge's deep analysis provided direction, linking growth-driving objectives to the $17 million goal.

Diane is smart and motivated, and with Steve's help, Diane:

1. Shared the equity value goal with the senior team,

2. Created a phantom stock plan through which the team could benefit from the value their work would create, promoting collaboration and loyalty,

3. Delegated authority with accountability to the team, and thereby to the goal,

4. Implemented a weekly flash report that promoted collaboration with accountability and tracked progress toward the goal (see also Dimension 1, Financial Reporting Processes),

5. Evolved into her proper role as the steward of shareholder value rather than the day-to-day operator, with a side benefit of making the business easier for her to run and improving her work/life balance, and

6. Instituted cross-functional collaboration and teamwork, while short- and long-term succession plans were put in place.

Imagine having this deep clarity as you design a client's execution project. Without it, the advisor and client are partially blind. With it they make informed decisions in logical sequence, creating a launchpad for growing profits and value and then lighting the rocket. High confidence, high ROI, with the groundwork done to deliver a win.

In the appendix of this book, you have questionnaires you can use to analyze your client's business alignment with the three dimensions of business growth's twenty-four growth-driving objectives. As seen above with Diane's business, if the answer becomes partly true, we need to find out what is missing.

RECAP

Deep business analysis generates total clarity about what's needed to get success. Effective analysis of strategic capacity should capture senior team consensus. The analysis dispassionately generates data (although the process may get passionate!) that is neither good news nor bad news. We can't get emotionally involved in the data. If we don't consider all the data, then we can't truly make informed decisions. The data needs to come from an open discussion by the people it's going to impact the most. This in turn allows the advisor to create a data-informed strategic growth project plan that can be delivered using the execution leadership system.

GOALS AND DATA FUEL STRATEGY

After reading this chapter, you will understand the link between strategic capacity in the context of the three dimensions of business growth and designing an executable strategy.

Why is strategic planning so important? The data tells us that almost 25 percent of businesses don't have a strategic plan, while experience tells us that the other 75 percent of businesses commonly have faulty, misconceived plans (that sometimes aren't plans at all).[22] When private equity purchases an enterprise, they immediately think thoroughly through a strategic plan and are rigorous about execution. Lacking a strategic plan is a growth killer, as well as an existential threat to transferable value.

Vision, mission, strategy. Before diving headfirst into this chapter, we should first make sure that certain words, terms, ideas, and concepts are clearly defined. When we as professionals hear "vision" or "strategy," different definitions may come to mind. When speaking with CEOs, they often use vision and mission and strategy inter-changeably, and this mistake can be fatal. We need a unifying and clear understanding of the language used within the growth-drive system.

---

22 Graham Kenny, "Your Strategic Plans Probably Aren't Strategic, or Even Plans," *Harvard Business Review*, April 6, 2018, https://hbr.org/2018/04/your-strategic-plans-probably-arent-strategic-or-even-plans.

First, vision. Vision is larger than the business. Using Growth-Drive LLC's vision as an example, their vision is to deploy the three dimensions of business growth to leave an indelible positive impact on one trillion dollars' worth of middle-market businesses.

Mission is a subset of the vision. What big things need to be true to move toward the vision? Let's keep using Growth-Drive LLC. Their mission is to invest business advisors with knowledge, tools, and support to move clients in the three dimensions of business growth. The mission statement helps deliver the vision.

Finally, strategy. Strategy is quite simply what we are going to do to win. For Growth-Drive LLC, the strategy is to be the business advisor's indispensable resource for winning and executing profit- and value-growth engagements. They must deliver the tools, training, and support advisors need to work with one trillion dollars' worth of businesses.

Let's hit these concepts again through the lens of a sports team. Ownership's vision might be to build a dynastic organization and win multiple successive sport championships (Super Bowl, Stanley Cup, World Series, etc.). The mission is to create a team that can win the first championship. The strategy is to attract and retain top talent. Tactics would then include free agency, drafting, coaching, building team culture, etc. Do you see how each builds into the next?

In the growth-drive system, one could say that for a client like Ridge Specialty Tooling,[23] business immortality is the vision. High strategic capacity is the mission. Reaching growth-driving objectives

---

23 "Ridge Specialty Tooling" is a fictitious company used here and in other growth-drive courses and supporting resources. To avoid confusion or association with real entities, we have performed searches using leading web browsers and GPT4 and confirmed that this is a unique name that to the best of our knowledge is not being used by others. Any similarity in name or facts is unintended and completely coincidental.

is the strategy. And running the execution leadership system is tactical. Ridge's "$3 million EBITDA" goal is a waypoint, not a destination, not a mission, and certainly not a strategy. We're stating the obvious because sometimes clients will say something like "Our strategy is to deliver $3 million of profit by the end of next year." See the disconnect?

Of course strategy cannot be created in a vacuum. Strategy is informed by strategic capacity. Looking back to chapter 3's focus on effective senior leadership, capacity is defined by the effectiveness of the senior leadership team, the productivity and loyalty and engagement of the workforce, and so on. Ridge has a vision and mission, and maybe as part of that mission, they have defined an interim strategic goal of reaching $3 million. Therefore, before we can craft strategy to reach this goal, we have to understand current strategic capacity or how the business measures up to best practices. Best practices are growth-driving objectives.

In this chapter we are going to focus on designing strategy using what you've learned leading the deep analysis of your client's business. In chapter 1, we discussed deep discovery and uncovering your client's growth goal. This growth goal defines where your client's enterprise needs to go. Now

> **Strategy defines how your client moves from their status quo to their goal. Reaching objectives and key results is the tactical work needed to execute the strategy.**

we'll explore strategy. Strategy defines how your client moves from their status quo to their goal. Reaching objectives and key results is the tactical work needed to execute the strategy. Think of strategy as having a map where X marks the growth goal, strategy is the path to X, and the OKRs are the steps along this path.

CREATING STRATEGY FROM ANALYSIS: REDESIGNING THE BUSINESS SO IT CAN WIN

We are moving into the last part of the analysis section, learning about extracting analysis information to fuel strategy. Remember, the analysis must create total clarity about what is needed to get success, to win. In this chapter we focus on the data extracted in the context of strategic thinking, strategic planning, and strategic doing. The goal is to answer these three questions:

- What is strategy, and why is strategy important for growth?
- What are the phases of strategic business planning?
- How do you integrate the growth-drive methodology and facilitation to fuel strategic planning?

In the three dimensions of business growth, strategy is Dimension 2's first growth-driving objective. We've discussed the importance of strategic execution for creating predictable profitable growth. Businesses following best practices for this objective must use a written strategy to execute their mission; the strategy must therefore deliver shareholder goals. So executing the strategic plan must make defined shareholder goals reality.

Understanding this process helps you to increase strategic capacity, thereby increasing predictability in all three dimensions. The process helps the business move from an aspirational vision to a tangible reality that can be mapped out through OKRs. The process flows management by objective (steps on the path), with objectives as part of a coordinated strategy (to reach X on the map), and tactical actions generating measurable results (walking from step to step). Let's explore how this process plays out.

WHAT IS STRATEGY?

Let's set the stage with a story about a client, a middle-market health-care business with $35 million a year in revenue. They've been successful, enjoying recurring and predictable revenue with positive customer and supplier relationships. Through their reputation, they've become established in their community. As a healthcare business founded and run by nurses, they take great pride in their clinical excellence and great people. This business started having issues before the outset of the COVID-19 pandemic, with some of their big referral sources abandoning them, along with losing some of their clinical expertise. Without a proper sales plan, their sales staff and manager started underperforming. With changing regulations in their marketplace, competition increased, and the business found itself under threat, looking for help.

The business found itself flat-footed in a changing market, stuck in the mud, and not profitable. The leadership and staff were emotional and frustrated. What their advisor recognized during discovery was that they lacked a strategic mindset, the ability to see the holistic playing field of the market, and therefore how to respond and plan around it. The client was not thinking in a transformational, strategic mindset. What their advisor did was to help them get unstuck by developing a strategic "can do, will do" mindset, incorporating the transformational mindset introduced in chapter 1. Getting into the right headspace is a huge win in this battle.

> **Developing a strategic mindset driving long-term growth requires a disciplined process.**

Developing a strategic mindset driving long-term growth requires a disciplined process. First, as advisors we need to ground ourselves in a common language. The dictionary definition of strategy can help us contextualize strategy within growth-drive. The root of the word is from the Greek *strategia*, "the art of the general" (or military commander), and is applicable in the business setting since the function of command is in the C-Suite, focused as it should be on creating and executing strategy. From this notion, let's define strategy as the choices we make to win.

Good strategic thinking, planning, and doing help you shape the long-term growth of your client's business. Good strategic thinking considers the market, competition, people, sales, and operations and also the trade-offs needed for implementation, specifically what is gained and lost by different options. The transformational mindset postulates all the possible outcomes of a given strategic path and works backward from there. Strategic thinking considers barriers to the execution of the plan, giving the business management key forewarning of icebergs threatening their ship. This is where it's vital to understand, and at times reinforce, your client's commitment to reaching their vision. The total clarity you've developed by correctly identifying your client's goals and commitment, plus the deep analysis you've led on their strategic capacity, creates transparency and unity of purpose. Done correctly, your client will be willing, able, and ready to execute the strategy. That was the case with the healthcare business described above.

Keep in mind that there is a flow to the process, helping us as advisors put tasks in doable "boxes" for our clients. These boxes are informed by incorporating OKRs into the strategy—business objectives that are going to drive strategic execution through tactical action.

Let's revisit the OKR system for goal design. OKRs are objectives and their supporting key results. Key results in a strategic plan are time bound, which creates accountability. Here's a great definition for a key result: "Key results benchmark and monitor how we get to the objective. Effective KRs are specific and time bound and aggressive yet realistic. Most of all, they are measurable and verifiable. You either meet a key result's requirements or you don't; there is no gray area, no room for doubt."[24]

Let's sharpen the spear: Best practice with OKRs is to add D. The D stands for discussed. One cannot overstate the power of transparency and alignment, and these are created and fostered by discussion, by communication. OKR-D is captured in growth-drive's strategic objective: "You document, are transparent about, and communicate your business's vision and mission, strategy, performance, SOPs, and culture both internally and externally" (emphasis added).

OKR-D helps the business reach goals. For Ridge, the goal is GR $33 million with 10 percent net income by the end of Plan Year Five. This goal is SMART: Specific, Measurable, Ambitious, Realistic, and Timely. And through Steve's coaching, this also became discussed. Specific? "$33 million at 10 percent margin," check. Measurable? Check. Achievable? We're talking here about having five years to double margin, bringing it into line with industry … check. Relevant? The goal delivers shareholder Diane's personal and professional goals, check. And time bound? Five years, check. Add D, discussed, and you now have transparency while promoting communication and collaboration. When you help your client define a business goal like this, you are then ready to define the strategy and tactics to achieve that goal.

Forewarned is forearmed: We are talking here about business owners. If you're a veteran advisor, the following will be painfully familiar; if you're new to the game, be mindful. When you ask a client, "What is your strategy?" they are going to give you a short explanation

---

24   Ryan Panchadsaram, "What Is an OKR? Definition and Examples," What Matters, accessed May 18, 2023, https://www.whatmatters.com/faqs/okr-meaning-definition-example.

THE GROWTH-DRIVING ADVISOR

of their primary goal or objective and what they see as the actions and activities necessary to move the enterprise in that direction. These broad generalities often do little to hold their senior team accountable, so our job as advisors is to get the leadership team focused on a set of OKR-Ds using the system described throughout this work.

WHY IS STRATEGY IMPORTANT FOR GROWTH?

One of the most important ideas your client must understand is "What got you here won't get you there." Recall the healthcare business discussed earlier. They did a beautiful job getting here but required profound changes to get to a future there. The strategic thinking conversation you've already led the client through has brought clarity to the there, to the goal, while the discovery conversation gave you a critical understanding of the client's here. If you do not know where you are going, any path will take you there.

Emotion: Clients will say things like "We are stuck," "I'm frustrated," "We are no longer growing," "We can't seem to break through," "My business is worth less than I thought," "How do we move from 3 percent growth to 15 percent growth?" When you hear these, listen for the emotion—that's your opportunity. When we talk about change, finding the emotional motivation and commitment to make positive change is among the most difficult steps. It has to be rooted in the client's emotional "Why?" for growth, with a compelling reason to make change. Use the growth conversation techniques.

The value of establishing clarity on the client's "Why?" is that it helps our clients first conceptualize a better future and provides the emotional bond needed to do the hard work required to make this future a reality. All the while the client will be using the three dimensions of growth framework to reduce risk and increase predictability of revenues and profits. Further the client will be more agile in response to changes in the market forces through their use of strategic and transformational mindsets. In short, it helps them define their purpose, their why, and it helps them make better decisions, understanding the trade-offs of their decision making. This will lead to better prioritizing the actions they are going to take.

Look back at the inverted pyramid describing commitment in chapter 1. Harnessing emotion and focusing on the true "Why?" allows you to maintain tempo, win battles, and ultimately win the war. Our job is to listen deeply, rising at opportunities to help the client better understand their own "Why?" and push them to find deeper motivation for growing the business. From here we use strategic planning to make the client's desired outcome a reality.

Most of the critical decisions to be made center around people and capital—at the end of the day, the only resources a business has. You want your client's management team to have an almost military perspective of knowing themselves, their people, their capital, and their processes. They also must know the competition and the market. Knowing themselves means having the data that provides total clarity about their strategic capacity. Of the twenty-four growth-driving objectives, eight concern people, and an additional seven focus on finance. Process is laced throughout, with six objectives being process specific. But let's be clear: the entire system is about integrated processes.

Another critical discussion is on trade-offs. Depending on the depth of where you are going, you may put it in terms of case scenarios. This allows the client to own it. Let them understand: If we do this, the best result we could get is X. Y is the expected result. And if we do this, the worst-case result is Z. They need to see the continuum to be able to make good trade-off decisions. Each case has assumptions and trade-offs that allow us to make better decisions. Use exercises for prioritizing decision making around what's most important and what's most urgent to help them make better decisions.

Recap: Ask each owner, "What is your business goal? How does that line up to your personal goal? What about your partners, the board? Your family?" If it's a family-owned business, you will often see a lot of misalignment among family members, often including people who are not even involved in the business but who have an emotional impact on the CEO. And what about the leadership team and their personal and professional goals? When we talk about growth and driving growth, we need to be clear around goal alignment. All of this informs strategy.

WHAT ARE THE PHASES OF STRATEGIC BUSINESS PLANNING?

There are five phases of strategic planning. Earlier we introduced the strategic mindset, using the words thinking, planning, and doing. The strategic mindset comes to life with the analyze, design, and execute phases of the growth-drive action cycle. Drawing parallels, strategic thinking falls under the analyze phase, strategic planning falls under the design phase, and strategic doing falls under the execute phase. Before these come two prep phases, as we'll see. When you teach your client the cycle, you are leading a quiet revolution within their organization, building strategic muscle to make the enterprise a competitive juggernaut. The strategic mindset should become unconscious and drive a strategic culture, a part of what the enterprise is. It creates the opportunity for you to help them in the long term.

While you are prioritizing and addressing growth-driving objectives, you are deciding which OKRs are the real bottlenecks to growth. Apply the three dimensions—these prioritize areas for action in line with the client's goals. You are always looking at decision-making trade-offs, watching cash like a hawk. And you're always looking at that willing, able, and ready component.

With personal and business goals defined, let's examine the phases of the strategic prep and planning process.

1. Where are we now? (Deep Analysis)

2. Where do we want to be? (Business and Personal Goals Aligned)

3. How will we get there? (Strategy)

4. What must we do to achieve that? (OKR Tactics)

5. How are we doing? (Constant Analysis against KPIs)

Think of the first two questions as part of the analysis. The third and fourth questions are connected to design. And the final question is execution.

Looking at a strategic plan road map, begin with "Where are we now?" This question will necessarily move the conversation into a discussion of strategic capacity to deliver predictable revenue, profits, and transferable value. Strategy also relies on financial analysis, leadership, owner dependence, the state of the market, and assessing both competency and alignment within the leadership team.

That leads to the next essential question, "Where do we want to be?" This should include a discussion on guiding principles (a.k.a. core values) and purpose, the why of the enterprise, with a defined destination vision aimed at growing the business and increasing its transferable value. When we are able to do that, we are able to better identify all the options and choices that might exist, leading us to the question, "How will we get there?"

"How will we get there?" encompasses the goals of the business, leading logically to concrete definitions of vision, mission, and strategy.

Throughout, we are integrating the growth-driving objectives and the cycle of analyze-design-execute.

HOW DO WE INTEGRATE THE GROWTH-DRIVE METHODOLOGY AND FACILITATION TO FUEL STRATEGIC PLANNING?

We do strategic planning in the context of applying it to the three dimensions of business growth to move up the pyramid. At face value almost all senior teams would describe themselves as collaborative, but truly collaborative management teams are rare. Partners can see their business goals differently. Any source of their angst and inability to collaborate as a team is rooted in not seeing the world the same way. How can you create an effective and executable plan in that environment? Without that initial discovery, you might be setting up for failure.

Here's how you might leverage the analysis of capacity in Dimension 1 to create strategy. The process is straightforward. Once you have a deep analysis of the business, you have scores for every objective and key result in the three dimensions of business growth. This is over 150 data points. Because you have also discovered the CEO or business owner's goals, you can prioritize these OKRs for action using the three dimensions. Strong OKRs are monitored during every analyze phase. Weak OKRs are prioritized for action in design and brought up to best-in-class standards using execute sprints. As a growth driver, you know that the first priority is to create predictable profits and cash flow, the launchpad for growing profits and transferable equity value.

We'll provide an explanation of each of the Dimension 1 growth-driving objectives and for the sake of space the key results for the effective senior leadership OKR. The whole nine yards is included in the appendixes and related online resources.

1. Effective leadership team: An effective leadership team plays a crucial role in creating corporate strategy. A strong leadership team ensures that the business can continue to run smoothly even in the absence of key individuals. This allows the company to focus on long-term goals, plan for growth and expansion, and maintain a competitive edge. Assuming your client isn't living up to best-in-class practices, here are the strategic steps you'll include in your plan to create an effective leadership team that is aligned with and accountable to the business's vision and mission, helping the shareholders achieve their objectives:

   ▫ *Challenge the shareholders to provide written time-bound goals for the business that are shared with the senior leadership team,*

   ▫ *Ensure that the senior leadership team understands and aligns with the shareholder goals,*

   ▫ *Use communication, compensation, and tools like a flash report to help the senior leadership be accountable to the business's vision, mission, and strategy and thereby to the shareholder goals,*

   ▫ *Communicate by deploying the execution leadership system, and senior leadership will begin to meet regularly to review and discuss progress toward the shareholder goals, and*

   ▫ *Use the techniques described in this work and the broader growth-drive system to delegate CEO authority to the senior team, helping them evolve to a point where the business runs smoothly in the CEO's absence.*

2. Productive and loyal employees: Productive and loyal employees are essential for a company's success. They help maintain high-quality standards and provide excellent customer service. This can result in increased customer satisfaction and repeat business, which lead to a high percentage of recurring revenues.

3. High percentage of recurring revenues: A high percentage of recurring revenues can be a sign of a successful business model. This indicates that the company has a loyal customer base and a sustainable revenue stream. It also reduces the risk of relying on one-off transactions, which can be unpredictable.

4. Gross and net margins above industry norm: Maintaining gross and net margins above industry norms is critical for long-term success. This allows the company to invest in growth, innovation, and research and development. Higher margins can also provide a buffer against economic downturns or unexpected expenses.

5. Strong financial reporting processes: Strong financial reporting processes are essential for corporate strategy. They help management make informed decisions based on accurate financial data. They also help identify areas of weakness and opportunities for growth.

6. Documented sales process: A documented sales process can help increase efficiency and effectiveness. This can lead to increased sales and revenue growth. It also ensures

consistency in sales performance and can help identify areas for improvement.

7. Documented operational processes: Documented operational processes are important for streamlining operations and increasing efficiency. This can lead to cost savings and improved profitability. It also ensures consistency in operations and can help identify areas for improvement.

8. Customer satisfaction tracking: Tracking customer satisfaction is critical for long-term success. It helps identify areas of strength and weakness and provides valuable feedback for improvement. It also helps ensure customer loyalty, which can lead to increased recurring revenues and referrals.

3 DIMENSIONS OF BUSINESS GROWTH

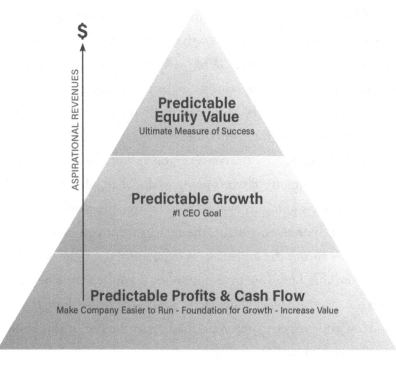

Where are we now? We've covered discovery of the shareholder goals and the business's strategic capacity. You've also seen that leadership nonalignment can be a growth killer, as are not having well-defined roles and responsibilities, failures of business culture, financial reporting issues, and more. All of these issues benefit from a facilitated discussion, and you are the facilitator. It involves having people tell stories, giving you insight through specific examples. It's not easy, but with training, practice, and coaching, most advisors become great at it. During the facilitation, you want to bring the leadership team to understand that alignment around goals, objectives, roles, and accountabilities must be well thought out, or execution of the strategic plan will most likely fail. As a side note and not to complicate matters, be vigilant for business/personal alignment and potential misalignment with partners, family members, and the board, which is a very real threat to layer on top of the leadership team's perspective and wishes.

Where does the client want to be? This is where you weave the three dimensions of business growth into your discussion. The three dimensions lead to asking, "What is it that you want to achieve, Madam CEO?" Does she want to make the business easier to run? Create sustainable growth? Monetize value? The growth conversation is magic at answering these questions.

From there, we have the conversation around the actual strategic plan, the mapping out of who's going to do what, why, how, and by when, and who's going to oversee and manage the plan's execution. You must include the oversight, the management coaching, and the feedback to ensure the execution is happening the right way. Then look at tracking how you are doing to see if your client is on target, and if not, why and what adjustments need to be made along the way.

How will we get there? Well, that's what the rest of this book is about, so stay tuned.

Before we go, let's look at an example of a technique for facilitating strategic planning. Have you ever done a strengths, weaknesses, opportunities, and threats (SWOT) analysis? Think about deep analysis as helping you identify external opportunities and threats to the client's business. Looking for the opportunities is an easier, more positive conversation. Market and operational strengths will define the client's ability to take advantage of opportunities. Then sift the strengths and the weaknesses from strategic capacity analysis data and feedback from senior leadership discovery conversations. Whenever you're reviewing results, be sure to show the client where they are strong. If you fixate just on the weakness, you run the risk of wearing your client down, so make sure you strike a balance between discussing strengths and opportunities before discussing weaknesses and threats. You need to keep them energized; recognizing their strengths does this. Keep those strengths front-of-mind as the links to the opportunities for the business. You'll use this same technique when you deploy the execution leadership system.

Remember to encourage your client to articulate their mission, including their purpose and their values, at the beginning of meetings. Have it put on cards and posted on walls. Not only is this part of the flow of good strategic facilitation, it is a hallmark of successful businesses.

Now let's add a few thoughts about implementation because that's strategic "doing." Best-of-breed businesses have an engaged workforce. You'll want to know that your client has the right people in the right positions and that senior leaders are facilitating, not dictating. As far as "doing the right things," function-mapping exercises are a terrific way to get off a 2D organization chart and into the real world, keeping the business from getting mired in charts and descriptions.

A few things to consider while you are actually implementing the process. You might have an authoritative owner or senior leader, making it harder to get the necessary input for good strategic planning to happen. It goes hand in hand with high owner dependency, a business that cannot run smoothly in the CEO's absence. Rather, at the senior leadership level we seek to achieve empowerment of employees to their full capabilities. You are assessing where the CEO is, plus levels of dependence in senior leadership, leadership culture within the organization, and more. How well are they aligned? Is the organization a smooth-running machine, or is there gravel in the gears?

Based on the input from our consulting colleagues, you might consult Porter's Five Forces in terms of the industry analysis and then look at a trend analysis. Then look at putting those together in strengths, weaknesses, and trends, which is the external view of the environment, and then narrow it down into SWOT, which we consider to be an internal analysis. For smaller businesses, it may not be as relevant as with bigger businesses.

Recap: As a consultant, you can either choose to begin by asking the client where they are now, then leading to "Where do you want to go?" Or you can look at where they want to go first. That creates excitement, opportunity, and momentum. That puts that CEO in that future world of his or hers and then gets them to look back and start talking about how they can get there. You would do this with the CEO, who certainly needs to be aligned with the rest of his team, before you go into the deep dive with the whole team. In terms of leadership, we can do an even deeper dive, and that may require some form of leadership assessment. Leadership drives everything in the business. You might look at something like Patrick Lencioni's Five Dysfunctions of a Team.

On another point, when we look at strengths, as giants Gino Wickman and Verne Harnish agree, we're helping our client be different. There's no value in being the same. When we are looking at our strength, we are looking for strength to enable us to be different. Wickman talks about "unique" as having at least one of our three unique points[25] that cannot be copied by anybody else. Nobody else has those exact three. These are something that we want to help the client identify, a conversation or workshop through which we deliver immediate value as a consultant using the growth-drive process. They don't often get into strategic thinking the way that we defined it, and they rarely if ever look at their entire operation. As CEOs, as operators, they are managing from bottleneck to bottleneck, often feeling stuck in a flywheel. The value you bring to the table involves opening the lens, stepping back, and saying, "Let's look at your processes and people in the context of your goal and sort out how we're going to redesign those processes and maybe the people, too, and move this business toward your goal." Then you use your clarity about how they score on objectives and key results to design a strategy that can win—that makes the goal a reality.

You've now completed the analysis phase of your engagement. You and your client have total clarity about where the client wants to go, what it means to them personally and professionally, and where the business is operationally, and you have a good feel for the alignment and ability of the senior leadership team. Now you can move into redesigning the business so that it can reach your client's goal. Welcome to design.

---

25   Gino Wickman, *Traction: Get a Grip on Your Business* (Dallas: BenBella Books, 2012).

DIMENSION 1 OF BUSINESS GROWTH

Predictable Profits & Cash Flow

After reading this chapter, you will understand the eight OKRs that must be in place to move a business from its status quo to delivering predictable profits and cash flow.

At this point in the engagement, you have moved from leading the growth conversation and establishing yourself as the guide to giving them total clarity about how the business measures up against the growth-driving objectives. By fully implementing Dimension 1, the client builds a sturdy launchpad for the growth of the business. As previously mentioned, each dimension consists of eight objectives and key results (OKRs), which when implemented bring the business in line with best practices. Having familiarized yourself in depth with the client's strategic capacity, it is time to move from analysis to design with a plan to move them from their status quo to their growth goal.

In chapter 2, you were given an overview of the three dimensions of business growth. Over the next three chapters, we will look at each dimension in detail. Let's start with Dimension 1, Creating Predictable Profits and Cash Flow.

Why predictable profits and cash flow? While predictable profits are great, you must have predictable cash flow as well. Helping the client establish predictable profits and cash flow is the prerequisite to any engagement where you want to create growing revenues and/or grow transferable value. When you've completed your analysis of the business, you will understand the strengths, weaknesses, opportunities, and threats (SWOT) either through that lens or through the lens of Growth-Drive's twenty-four OKRs, being able to elaborate on the key strengths, weaknesses, opportunities, and threats facing the business. Strength in key areas adds resilience to your client's launchpad for growing the business, allowing

> **Strength in key areas adds resilience to your client's launchpad for growing the business, allowing for growth with greater predictability and less chaos.**

for growth with greater predictability and less chaos. Importantly, any increase in predictability of profits and cash flow makes a business easier to run while increasing value at current revenues, potentially to the top end of the range of multiples for the industry.

Cash is lifeblood. Too often cash gets caught in the balance sheet. Here's a real-world case. There was a high-end luxury goods manufacturer. The enterprise was oblivious to their flawed business model, as they never took time to step back and get clarity on the bigger picture. They would take a deposit to start an order and collect the balance upon delivery. Although on paper the margin from the deposit was more than sufficient to fund the cost of goods, the model did not account for growth or delays in manufacturing. The P&L showed profits, but delays in delivery locked up cash in inventory. The business's cash was caught in the balance sheet, right between the P&L and the cash flow statement. As a result, the cash ratio was off; it was a net negative. Over time, compounded with a dip in demand during the 2008 recession, the negative cash became a fatal flaw, and the business went under.

Your client needs to have a clear understanding of their cash flow in order to make it predictable. We encourage you to sit down with your client and help them understand what a cash flow statement looks like and how to read it. Give them a copy of Berman and Knight's excellent *Financial Intelligence*,[26] and highlight the sections they should read. Remarkably, few have any idea how to even read such a statement. Having your client read the statement is not enough. They need to track their cash flow weekly. The best practice is to prepare, share, and discuss a flash report that includes cash and other key metrics. When you sit with a client, you have to make sure they understand that they cannot manage a business by looking at a checkbook. They need to look beyond the P&L and the checking account. Dimension 1 is the launchpad for growth, and this free cash flow (FCF) is the fuel for the next dimension.

To fuel growth your client must generate more cash than they are burning. If we're looking down the road at the number one CEO goal, growing the business, know that growth can be shockingly expensive. In HBR's *Financial Intelligence*, the authors make the point that the businesses most able to invest in growth will be those that can generate their own cash.[27] This organic cash is the excess cash generated from operations without enlisting the help of debt and equity markets. In an assumed baseline market state, the business may have a line of credit (LOC) to dip into that requires repayment periodically. This shorter-term loan is meant to augment dips in cash flow as a crutch, not an artificial limb. You need to make sure that you help the CEO create a business that will invest in its own growth from its own organic cash, not from the LOC.

---

26   Karen Berman and Joe Knight, *Financial Intelligence: A Manager's Guide to Knowing What the Numbers Really Mean (Boston:* HBR Press, 2013).

27   Karen Berman and Joe Knight, *Financial Intelligence: A Manager's Guide to Knowing What the Numbers Really Mean (Boston:* HBR Press, 2013).

Once you've led the implementation of Dimension 1, you will have helped build a business that is well run, with highly predictable cash flow and low risk to continuing operations. Dimension 1 businesses make great businesses in which to invest for the future. If your client comes to you (as they will 62 percent of the time) and says, "I want to grow my business," you need to establish the Dimension 1 launchpad before rapid and dynamic growth through Dimensions 2 and 3.

Let's look at Dimension 1 and the eight objectives that must be reached to drive predictable profitable revenue growth.

	GROWTH DRIVER	BEST PRACTICE	OBJECTIVES
1	Effective Senior Leadership	You have an effective leadership team, and the business can run smoothly in your absence.	Your business has an effective leadership team that is aligned with and accountable to the business's vision and mission, helping the shareholders achieve their objectives.
2	People: Productive and Loyal	Your employees are productive and loyal.	Every employee and contractor understands their role and the metrics defining their success, both individually and for their team contributing to the business's goals.
3	High Percentage of Recurring Revenue	You have a high percentage of recurring revenues.	Your business can predict a significant portion of future revenue from customers through contracts or other means.
4	Strong Margins	You generate gross and net margins above the industry norm.	Your business has a history of gross and net margins greater than the industry norm.
5	Financial Reporting Processes	You have strong financial reporting processes.	You regularly prepare and share P&L, balance sheet, and cash flow reports, and weekly you prepare, distribute, and discuss flash reports tracking the key metrics needed to analyze and predict business performance as a tool for reaching business goals.

6	Scalable Sales Process	You use a documented sales process.	You have a documented sales process with a proven track record of success that is universally applied and scalable.
7	Strong SOPs	You have documented operational processes.	Your business has strong, documented standard operating processes that ensure consistent successful delivery on the promises made to the marketplace by sales.
8	High Customer Satisfaction	You track customer satisfaction.	Your business routinely measures customer satisfaction and uses this information to manage and improve performance.

As you take a holistic approach to analyzing, designing, and executing, you will avoid falling into the trap of working on one area out of context. Every growth-driving objective is a gear, turning in concert with the other gears within the business engine. Delivering the eight OKRs for Dimension 1 creates a business that is easier to run, making the 21 percent of CEOs who want operational freedom happy. To the extent that Dimension 1 impacts value capacity, it also increases value at current revenues. You will have created the launchpad from which to attack Dimensions 2 and 3. You need to think about these growth-driving objectives within the total context of all three dimensions, remembering their characterization as gears and dimensions, not disconnected phases.

Let's start our discussion at the bottom of the stack with customer satisfaction. Why? Because a satisfied customer base is a hallmark of a well-run business. In order to increase customer satisfaction, almost every other Dimension 1 growth-driving objective needs to be functioning at or near industry bests. Customer satisfaction is akin to dark matter[28] inside the business. Deciding to create high customer satisfaction motivates strength in most of the other Dimension 1 OKRs.

So what's the magic behind creating satisfied customers? First, the sales team is going to tell potential customers exactly what they are going to get and why the product or service is better than the competition. Second, you ensure that you sell products and services at a price that your customers embrace. Your goal here is to create customer evangelists, telling anyone who will listen about how great your products and services are and how happy they are to be associated with your business. In essence you create high customer satisfaction by having the sales team set the right expectations about the products and services, and in turn, operations will then delight the client during the delivery. Timely and accurate delivery on the promises made to the market by sales generates customer evangelists. That is going to lend itself to strengthening the brand, a growth-driving objective in Dimension 3.

When you have satisfied customers, you may be able to start increasing the value that you charge for your products and services, driving up margin and increasing cash flow. Satisfied customers are more likely to come back and purchase from you again, generating recurring revenues. A strong recurring revenues gear is going to make the sales process easier. Your sales team now has an installed base of people to whom they can go for repeat revenues and referrals. You can see how these all start working together—it's a coordinated group of growth and equity value drivers. Working together these gears create a business that has predictable profits and cash flow. Remember, we are not even talking about growth yet, rather, making the same amount of money as today but with decreased chaos and increased profitability,

---

28   Dark matter is an invisible form of matter that is believed to make up approximately 85 percent of the matter in the universe. Its existence is inferred from its gravitational effects on visible matter, such as galaxies and stars.

allowing your client an increased level of operational freedom and improved quality of life. Rounding it out, senior leadership must be aligned with business goals and collaborating as a team, accountable for strength in each of these areas.

Now imagine a business with a highly satisfied customer base, generating recurring revenues with a well-understood sales process. Operations are delivering, without the usual chaos of trying to keep up with disconnected sales and marketing teams. Imagine what your client, whether business owner or CEO, will think when you have helped them make this a reality.

Let's discuss each of the Dimension 1 OKRs in a little more detail.

SENIOR MANAGEMENT

Objective: Your business has an effective leadership team that is aligned with and accountable to the business's vision and mission, helping the shareholders achieve their objectives.

Let's start with senior leadership. We previously referred to the difference between a collaborative team and a collegial team. Collegial is easy: as social animals, we like to get along. We avoid tense, fractious work environments. It's also true that leaders are better for business than mere managers because a great senior leadership team is the source of an effective, accountable business culture. You need a team that works effectively together, aligned with the business goals while collaborating to achieve them. Further, they should be accountable to each other and to the business goals, engaging in constructive criticism as well as leveraging strengths. Collaborative and accountable means the difference between stagnating and winning.

To give you an example, have you read Patrick Lencioni's *The Advantage*? I was hired by the CEO of the business that might well

THE GROWTH-DRIVING ADVISOR

have been "The Noah's Ark Management Team" cautionary tale.[29] Our telecom business grew revenues from a little more than $20 million to a little under $60 million in just four years through organic growth and two acquisitions. My role was to research and develop new go-to-market strategies that would maintain and expand our relevance as telecom moved from copper to the internet.

The two strategic acquisitions were of competitors we had defeated in the market. We made the acquisitions in order to get their call centers and customer installed bases, but the CEO also agreed to keep their senior managers. Our business was already chaotic, and doubling then tripling management headcount (with defeated enemies) was a body blow. Rather than embracing a transformational mindset and collaborating to redesign the business and make a massive business model jump to keep pace with the market, it quickly devolved into a "who moved my cheese" bar fight. You've already guessed the result: The business tanked, failing its customers, employees, and stake-holders. A lean, collaborative, and accountable senior team working together toward a vision, mission, and strategy would probably have prevented this catastrophe (the CEO and I discussed this a couple of years later), but the execs were more worried about winning for themselves than winning as a team.

The lesson is clear. Senior leaders need to work effectively together to deliver business objectives in line with the growth goal, and the growth goal should just be a milestone on the road to something bigger—the mission and vision. This all starts with clearly defined roles and accountability to executing strategy through reaching sequential objectives. The mission tells senior leaders that they are part of something bigger. When they get this, what happens? "Reaching

---

29   Patrick Lencioni, *The Advantage* (San Francisco: Wiley, 2012), 23.

$33 million GR with 10 percent net income in five years" creates a machine whose growth is sustainable past the goal.

Mistakes are normal. So is failure. A business cannot deliver high strategic capacity without both a tolerance for mistakes and the collaborative spirit and transparency to learn from them. Little secrets, fiefdoms, and petty jealousies destroy collaboration. Most senior leaders think about their department and not the company. Diane Ridge at Ridge Specialty Tooling has a team of five department leaders. What happens when they come to meetings focusing on "How does this project impact my department?" rather than "How can I help make this project a success?" Better to focus on how they can contribute to the project—regardless of whether it's

> **A business cannot deliver high strategic capacity without both a tolerance for mistakes and the collaborative spirit and transparency to learn from them.**

outside their department—for the betterment of the business as a whole. Well-run businesses are transparent, with clear communication and collaboration among the senior team. Senior leadership needs to be aligned with the business vision, mission, and strategy. Then discussion of objectives among the senior team will promote further alignment and collaboration.

Everyone needs to understand his or her role in turning those objectives into reality and work together in a coordinated fashion. This also leads to helping the shareholders reach their objectives. Remember, the business was started to create value, not to create a job. At the end of the day, the CEO needs to create value for the shareholder(s), even if they are one and the same. We want to hold them accountable and to change the way they run the business. Don't allow the CEO or senior leadership to hold their cards too close so others don't know what they have. Share the data. Regularly discuss and review progress. This can go to the rhythm of meetings and the ninety-day cycle (discussed in execution).

A critical concept to hammer into your client's head: In managing a business, there is no good news or bad news, there is only data. Be dispassionate, discuss mistakes, learn from them. Even celebrate them. Weakness in generating and using data is one of the biggest barriers to growth. Think back to when we led the growth conversation with the CEO, patiently distilling business and personal goals. Sharing the goals from this conversation with the senior team helps create alignment to the goals. Fostering collaboration is a logical extension of this conversation. Recall the architect–general-contractor–tradesperson framework discussed in chapter 1. The architect delivers the strategic growth project plan. The general contractor holds senior leadership accountable as they execute the plan. An organization that clearly understands goals and accountability will have teams that function effectively. How do you evaluate how the client's senior leaders, teams, and individuals are doing? The answer is to introduce success metrics and key performance indicators, which we'll explore in chapter 9.

PEOPLE: PRODUCTIVE AND LOYAL

Objective: Every employee and contractor understands their role and the metrics defining their success, both individually and for their team contributing to the business's goals.

With the senior team's head on straight, you widen the lens and focus on the employees and contractors serving the business. We live in a gig economy, with contractors and fractional talent playing a vital role, so they are necessarily included in our planning. Predictable profits and cash flows require a stable and productive workforce. That word "stable" is critical, as both acquiring and losing talent is expensive and disruptive.

But we also need to go beyond "stability," which is passive, and set our objective as creating and maintaining "loyalty," which is active. Loyalty derives from many sources, including a strategic culture (see Dimension 2). Loyalty derives from having compensation and benefits at or above industry norms. And loyalty is driven by the dignity of knowing you are making a contribution and are successful in your role.

This ties in with "productive." What is the day-to-day experience for an employee who doesn't have a clear understanding about whether or not they are successful? Does it help people to be responsible for their defined role if they can succinctly define what it means for them to be successful in their role within the context of the organization? How does it help if they have one number that defines their success? People thrive when they understand the metrics by which their performance is being viewed and measured. Having a job where you feel valued and productive creates dignity (and therefore loyalty). When employees know what they need to do, how their success is defined, what they mean in the context of the business, and what business success means for them, you'll have developed the critical components of

> **A positive strategic culture is critical to growth.**

a strategic culture. A positive strategic culture is critical to growth. By getting the People: Productive and Loyal question right during Dimension 1, you are reinforcing the launchpad from which to grow.

A note about innovation, which is a high-priority growth driver in Dimension 2. In the spirit of the interconnected gears in the business engine, how can we leverage creating innovation as a tool to promote loyalty? Consider this idea: What would happen if you told employees they can invest up to 10 percent of their work time to study and learn, to attend webinars, etc.? At just four hours a week, this time is a great way to make sure people are able to go out and get new ideas.

It's also a great way to retain quality people. It's part of making sure that employees know you are interested in their growth personally and professionally. Businesses should consider adding nonremunerative mechanisms for retaining quality people. By the way, what do you think is one of the first things employees will tell family and friends about their job? You guessed it, they'll talk about this 10 percent.

Loyalty and productivity can be supported with profit-sharing plans. These can be a good idea for certain businesses and situations, but whether or not they are a good fit depends on a variety of factors. There are advantages and disadvantages to consider:

Advantages:

- Encourages teamwork and motivation: By linking a portion of employees' compensation to the success of the company, profit-sharing plans can motivate employees to work together toward common goals.

- Increases employee loyalty: When employees have a stake in the company's success, they may be more likely to stick around for the long term.

- Can be a tax-efficient way to compensate employees: Depending on how the plan is structured, profit-sharing contributions may be tax-deductible for the employer and tax-deferred for the employee.

Disadvantages:

- Can be complex to administer: Setting up and administering a profit-sharing plan can require significant time and resources.

- May not be suitable for all types of businesses: Profit-sharing plans may not make sense for start-ups or companies that have irregular or unpredictable profits.

- May not be effective in achieving desired outcomes: If the profit-sharing plan is not structured properly, it may not have the desired effect of motivating employees or increasing loyalty.

While compensation can be a driver in today's economy, culture (another growth driver in Dimension 2) helps create a productive and loyal workforce. For example, one of our members works with an affiliate of Habitat for Humanity. Each person in leadership of that business makes $20,000–$30,000 less than if they worked elsewhere with the same skill set and experience. The mission, the culture, and the relationships keep them there. If those go away, so might these leaders.

Of course, clearly understood roles and success metrics must support business goals. When you break goals into objectives and objectives into key results, you can assign the key results to teams and further to individuals. This can create a functional extension of the organizational chart that more closely mirrors the real world, promoting collaboration and accountability.

HIGH PERCENTAGE OF RECURRING REVENUES

Objective: The business can predict a significant portion of future revenue from customers through contracts or other means.

When it comes to predictable profit and cash flow, let's set a high bar: What if 80 percent of revenues come from recurring sources? As an example, let's look at the restaurant industry. At first blush there doesn't seem to be an easy path to guarantee folks will come back beyond delivering good food and services (i.e., high customer satisfaction). One of our members was working with a celebrity chef's restaurant group in New York, and the owners developed a system of reviewing credit card receipts in order to distinguish frequent customers from newcomers. The first group was sent gift cards for a free bottle of wine, valet parking vouchers, etc. In New York, a valet voucher is a commodity since just parking the car can add $50–$70 to a night out. Unsurprisingly, this became an affinity program with clear KPIs that could be tracked over time: "How do we make sure the Smiths eat in one of our restaurants two, three, even four times a month?" This is a clearly defined and time-bound goal. And in this case, the creative solution worked wonders.

Recurring revenues are further supported when the customer base has a spread of new and long-term customers (Dimension 2 OKR). Do you hear customer satisfaction creeping in here? How do we move from a new customer to a stable customer, to increasing their spending with us as a satisfied customer who is with us for the long haul? Try articulating in a written document why customers will continue to buy from the business. Think about the impact satisfied customers have on recurring revenues.

Now some service industries operate without contracts. A business owner may say, "We don't have contracts, but 70 percent of our business is recurring, year after year, and turnover is very low." This is the case for example with lawn care and pest control. In addition, new business is derived from existing customers via word of mouth or a referral campaign that the organization undertakes.

When you deal with businesses and services, and that even includes lawyers and accounting firms, get them to talk about sources of new customers and whether this new demand has an impact on existing customers. Ask them about customer satisfaction—do customers tend to stay around? Do they know what other services are available? Has your client ever analyzed the lifetime value of the typical client? Classified them? Looked at profitability by class? These exercises help both identify not only the most loyal customers (recurring revenue), but also the deadweight that can either be solicited for new services or invited to do business elsewhere. Focusing on the recurring revenue generators with affinity programs can be transformative.

If you look at the automobile industry, what's the number one reason why dealerships keep contacting customers after their purchase of a car from them? The service business! Most of all their goal is to make sure you buy your next vehicle from them again and allow them to service your current vehicle. Think in terms of the lifetime value of an automobile customer, which by one estimate is between $650,000 and $1 million. And the cost of vehicles keeps escalating.

Remember the "three uniques" and encourage your client to reach outside their industry for fresh ideas that might increase the percentage of recurring revenue.

STRONG MARGINS

Objective: The business has a history of gross and net margins greater than the industry norm.

Margin is critical to predictable profits and cash flow. Think about what goes into increasing prices delivering more margin. First, operations must be effective and efficient in order to deliver high quality at relatively low cost. Second, the business must sell on value, that is, highlighting the direct benefits the product or service will yield the customer. Our advisors have proven that the businesses that sell their products and services based on value (rather than price) end up selling their businesses for higher multiples. Margin improvement increases both growth capacity and value capacity.

> **Margin improvement increases both growth capacity and value capacity.**

Clients often don't know where their margins should be. Help them understand industry, niche, and local norms. A documented process for monitoring and increasing margin also helps clients increase cash flow. Operational inefficiencies or lower-than-market pricing needs to be corrected, which creates new organic cash.

Margin destruction is also common. When asked why their margins are declining, clients often will throw out lots of reasons: my competitors are lowering their prices; my clients are pushing back on my prices; if I don't do something, I will lose business, which then leads to layoffs, etc. This happens even when the client knows they have weak margins, thinking the only way to stay competitive is to lower prices. If the business doesn't have margins at or above industry norms, find out why—job one—and help them fix it.

There should be a written policy that helps the client stay strong on their pricing. This applies to the sales team, to operations, to customer support—it applies everywhere. The policy is not only about having a pricing strategy that promotes selling on value, but also policies about discounting and promotions, reimbursements, the cost of processing sales (credit card and similar fees), and so on. If SOPs allow the business to deliver to spec faster than the competition, create a premium service and charge for it. Does the brand promise cheap, or does the brand promise quality? Quality is value. There are opportunities to increase margin throughout the business, and many small changes can add up to a big impact.

One advisor reports that 90 percent of the small businesses with whom they work underprice themselves. He suggested to a manufacturing company to raise prices by 20 percent. The client almost fell out of their seat, but further discussion led to a price increase of 17 percent. The business did not lose a single customer. To further push the issue, sometimes clients need to understand that not all business is good business. Maybe they need to let go of those clients who price shop. They may fear that the loss in business will lead to scaling back on labor. And then they wonder what happens if they stay strong on margins, get a lot of work, and then need to hire their workers back. This is toxic thinking. You generally shouldn't carry operational costs that are a drag on profitability just in case new orders come in. Deal with the need for additional capacity when needed, not prophylactically. Flash reports will help anticipate future capacity needs.

How do you help your client? First, you research and determine what the normal margins are for their industry. The growth-drive key results for margin are straightforward—gross margin advantage relative to both the industry and direct competitors, same for net margin. Add to this the key result, "The business can state three reasons it can defend forecasts of future gross and net margins at or above its industry and niche," and you've added a forward-looking tool as well.

To explain in simpler terms, the client needs to sell the same goods or services as their competitors while delivering them for the same or lower cost. Remember: Always keep an eye on customer satisfaction. Gross net margin within industry norms is good. Above industry norms is great. Margin is the glue between predictable profits and cash flow. Maintaining these profits and cash flow sustainably above the industry norm is the key link between revenues and transferable value. Strengthen Dimension 3 transferable value by improving Dimension 1 margins.

FINANCIAL REPORTING PROCESSES

Objective: Regularly prepare and share P&L, balance sheet, and cash flow reports. Weekly prepare, distribute, and discuss flash reports, tracking the key metrics needed to analyze and predict business performance as a tool for reaching business goals.

You have to live the numbers to control the numbers. You and the senior team need to understand exactly what is happening on a profitability basis. Further, transparency among the senior team is critical. Ask yourself: How many of your clients are managing their business finances based on their personal tax burden? They play with their financial results to minimize their taxes. And following this line of thinking, since corporate profits and personal income are taxed, they play games to avoid taxes. This type of thinking actually shoots accurate financial reporting in the foot; we'll get into the lethal impact these games have on value later (for most industries, value is a multiple of profit). The absence of accurate and timely financial reports is one of the top growth killers and further contributes to the value gap and related wealth gap. There is no transferable value without accurate and timely financial reports that can be suited or otherwise tested during a transaction.

Having a high level of confidence in our understanding of the client's free cash flow, as well as measuring and understanding margin, comes from strong financial and operating reports, specifically flash reports. As will be discussed in more detail, flash reports are a dashboard or scorecard for the business that effectively links operational processes with financial results. Think of flash reports as a way to track the business engine and to predict financial results. It stands to reason that the flash report will only be as useful as its data is accurate. Where the business owner/leaders are playing games with the numbers, they are combining bad data with good.

Let's circle back to effective senior leadership, transparency, accountability, and collaboration. Remember how we discussed the need for transparency? How can the senior team maximize its effectiveness if the CEO keeps the data to themselves, refuses to share financial information, and plays games with the numbers? It isn't easy to change old habits, but change they must. Hence getting the can-do/will-do confirmation as a qualifier early in the process.

This lack of transparency on financial performance coupled with tax games may be why flash reports are a drastically underutilized tool in middle-market businesses. Many actually do not have a clue what a flash report is. A budget is not a flash report, and a budget is not a plan. They need to report and discuss performance using timely and accurate data.

What does the client need for this OKR? An accurate profit and loss (P&L) statement based on a chart of accounts that follows industry norms. They'll need the P&L and balance sheet by the tenth of the following month. Early in the engagement they should get a cash flow report by noon on the first business day of each week; as financial reporting processes evolve, they will get the flash report, which includes cash, on this same weekly tempo. Most of all they need to have a working understanding of their three financial reports.

Not every number tracked has a dollar sign with it. A business with predictable profits and cash flow should be able to track things like lead quantity and quality at each stage of the sales process. You should know the cost of each qualified lead, which implies we have a quantified definition for the stages of the sales process. These are factors our client must understand if they are going to create predictability in their financial outputs and a forecast of cash required to run the business. There is nothing more stressful to a business owner than cash crunches. If we have predictable profits and cash flow, the cash crunch is a thing of the past.

SCALABLE SALES PROCESS

Objective: Have a documented sales process with a proven track record of success that is universally applied and scalable.

We need to document the sales plan to deliver the business's revenue goals. The business must have a defined process plus clear communication and understanding of the sales plan, especially among the sales team. And the sales team needs to make active use of up-to-date customer relationship management (CRM) software. The CRM should serve as a central source of truth about prospective, current, and former customers. The CRM is every bit as important as the financial reporting program. In a nutshell, a well-defined sales process is key to creating predictable cash flow.

Senior leadership needs to use and understand the CRM to discern why and when customers do (and don't) purchase products and services from the business. A CEO may proudly state that the sales team hits their number every month. Ask that CEO how they do it, and they look back at you like a deer in headlights. Moreover, as is the case with Diane Ridge, the CEO may be the top salesperson, which is fine for now but not for the long-term health of the company. Define, create a quantified process, delegate with accountability, and track dollars as they flow through the sales process.

> A well-defined sales process is key to creating predictable cash flow.

STRONG STANDARD OPERATING PROCESSES (SOPs)

Objective: Strong, documented standard operating processes that ensure consistent successful delivery on the promises made to the marketplace by sales.

Operations must deliver on the promises made to the market by sales and do so on time and to spec. This links sales with customer satisfaction, helping recurring revenues and brand. Work hard to write it all down. Interview. Question. Follow. Process map. Function map employees and the departments that need and feed strong SOPs. Make your client focus with all their energy to understand their SOPs and to understand them clearly and completely before they tinker with the machine. Follow the Hippocratic oath: First, do not harm. Measure twice and cut once. I think we've made the point. Assuming the machine is working well enough, guide your client to resist the urge to tinker. Redesign, execute, and test. It is imperative for this OKR that accurate and timely data is collected, shared, and discussed weekly and in daily team huddles in line with the execution leadership system.

For certain industries strong SOPs deliver revenue recognition, which goes straight into the P&L and generates cash. Strong SOPs are a priority for predictable cash flow and are a backbone for growth, and increasing sales will stress this objective. They are a high-priority OKR for the 21 percent of CEOs who want to make their business easier to run, are do-or-die for that number one CEO goal "growth," and contribute directly to high value capacity.

HIGH CUSTOMER SATISFACTION

Objective: The business routinely measures customer satisfaction and uses this information to manage and improve performance.

We've woven customer satisfaction into several of the preceding OKRs. Customer satisfaction is the dark horse of Dimension 1. As discussed earlier, to get this growth-driving objective right, a business must first do lots of other things right. Customer satisfaction drives predictable profits and cash flow, for your clients as much as for your own advisory business. It's like the timing gear in the business engine. It creates repeat customers, and it creates evangelists promoting your client's products and services. It may also allow them to charge premium pricing.

Here is a prime example of this principle in action. An aircraft parts supplier always delivered the spec, but they couldn't deliver on time. In fact, they had a better record on spec (delivering parts within dimensional and operational specifications) than the industry norm. But because they struggled to deliver within accepted industry time, they had to rely on price to drive sales and had to tell customers, "If you can wait, we'll deliver perfect parts and do it more cheaply." Working with a senior advisor, they were able to identify, isolate, and fix the bottlenecks to delivery. They figured out the time aspect and created a process through which they could deliver not only on time, but 65 percent faster than their competitors. Deliveries could now, at the same cost, be delivered ahead of time and guaranteed to spec. What did they do? They could now compete on quality and timeliness and create a premium service. They took their delivery time from twelve weeks down to two weeks. The market's expectation was six weeks, so they said, "We will deliver in six weeks. If you would like the two-week option, you will pay X more." This is pure margin, at no additional cost to their business. The result: they managed to take operational efficiency and turn it into a premium service for which they increased the margin, and that went right to the bottom line.

Fantastic customer satisfaction and premium pricing are your objectives. Documented customer satisfaction goals that are communicated internally and externally should be a number on the wall in the lobby. Develop and execute a plan to meet your customer satisfaction objectives.

RECAP

There are eight growth-driving objectives that are fundamental to building a successful business. By prioritizing these objectives, you can create a well-oiled machine that operates smoothly and achieves its goals. It is important to remember that these objectives are interconnected and must be viewed holistically rather than in isolation. Each objective is like a gear that must work in harmony with the others for the engine to run smoothly.

As you read through the list of objectives, you may find that some are more relevant to your clients' businesses than others. However, best practice is to consider all of them carefully, as they all play an important role in driving predictable profits and cash flow, providing the launchpad for growth. For instance, attaining high customer satisfaction is a crucial objective that depends on success in most of the other objectives. By prioritizing customer satisfaction, you can create a customer base that is loyal, which in turn can drive recurring revenue and improve margins. Think about the growth-driving objectives and how they can help your clients. By prioritizing these objectives, you can achieve operational freedom and increased value, and create a well-run business that is set up for success.

DIMENSION 2 OF BUSINESS GROWTH

Predictable Sustainable Growth

After reading this chapter, you will understand the eight objectives that must be reached to move a business from its status quo to delivering predictable profitable growth.

Dimension 2 builds on the launchpad you created with Dimension 1 OKRs. We have discussed creating predictable profits and cash flow. Now we will address the strategic steps for helping the 62 percent of CEOs who want to grow by discussing how to harness profits and cash flow to create predictable, profitable, and sustainable revenue growth.

As we have indicated, growth is expensive. Most businesses fund growth from organic cash. Predictable cash flow allows these businesses to pay for investments in people, marketing, and inventory—the delivery process needed to create sustainable growth. We are going to contrast sustainable growth with disorganized, chaotic growth, which can be very disruptive to an organization. As you recall, we mentioned that in the analysis conversation. Most CEOs think that if they double or triple their revenue, they will solve all their problems. While that can be true, more often than not, growth (especially without a strategic plan) creates chaos and stress inside the organization. This is because when the gears aren't really meshed together and working well, it creates friction that can lead to chaos. Remember, Dimension 1 is your touchstone: Quarterly (and during every analyze phase of the growth cycle), go back and make sure that those foundational OKRs remain strong.

Planning and process can prevent chaos. For instance, by investing in marketing today, a business cannot expect the marketing to deliver revenues immediately. But the new marketing effort may produce leads that are handed off to sales. Is sales ready? If sales converts the leads to customers, is operations ready? New leads need to be handed to productive salespeople; new sales employees may take upward of one year to become fully productive. Until then they are a negative cash flow. Does the plan account for all of this? Before a well-trained and experienced advisor comes on the scene, the answer is typically no. But with patience and planning, you will help your clients maximize their return on investment (ROI) with incremental dollars of new revenue and exponential dollars of transferable value.

The following lists Dimension 2's eight growth-driving objectives, which must be reached to drive predictable profitable revenue growth.

	GROWTH DRIVER	BEST PRACTICE	OBJECTIVES
1	Strategic Vision, Planning, and Execution	You have a written vision, mission, and strategy.	You document, are transparent about, and communicate your business's vision, mission, strategy, performance, SOPs, and culture both internally and externally; you have the capacity to execute.
2	Strategic Culture	You have a strong culture that you actively nurture.	Your business culture helps deliver your vision, mission, and strategy.
3	People: Hiring and Training	You can easily hire and train new employees.	You have a documented and effective process to hire, onboard, and train people that has a proven record of creating productive and loyal contributors to the business's success.

4	Large Market Size	Your market supports significant growth of your business.	Your market supports significant growth of the business including one or more of the following: geographic opportunities, diversifying revenues from current customers, noncannibalizing new sales, and strategic acquisitions.
5	Unique Products/ Services	Your products and services are unique.	Your products/services have unique characteristics that allow you to sell on value not price.
6	Scalable Marketing Process	You use a documented marketing process.	Your business can produce leads in a proven and systematic way, ensuring adequate potential customers at each stage of the buyer's journey.
7	Financial: Budget, Forecast, Actuals	You manage the business using a budget.	You manage finances using a budget and forecasts and have a documented history of actual financial performance at or above forecast.
8	Innovation Creates a Competitive Advantage	You foster innovation in every area of the business.	Your business understands the value of innovation and has a proven and systematic way to drive and capture innovation from employees, vendors, customers, and the market at all levels and for every area of the business.

STRATEGIC VISION, PLANNING, AND EXECUTION

Objective: You document, are transparent about, and communicate your business's vision, mission, strategy, performance, SOPs, and culture both internally and externally; you have the capacity to execute.

Why should clients grow using a plan? Because growing a business without a plan leads to chaos. Of course, chaos can exist without growth, but chaos can become destructive when growth is not planned or managed. Believe it or not, businesses can grow to death. An effective strategy couples goals, such as target revenue, with strategic capacity.

Imagine Dimension 1 creating a stream of cash. Where can this cash take us? Will the cash be spent (burned) or invested? Having a plan helps ensure that the cash is invested, using defined success metrics. And where are we going? What

Growing a business without a plan leads to chaos.

are the strategic vision, mission, strategy, and objectives? Do we have a culture of growth where every employee understands where the business is going and their individual part in getting it there? Do they have a culture of innovation, of growth, of delighting the customer? Is there even a market into which to grow? All of these questions need answers.

The answers come from research and discovery. The answers allow the CEO and their advisor to define SMART goals. As we've seen, having goals and data is part of the equation. We also need a strategic plan and the capacity to execute the plan. The business needs to have what it takes to make the goals reality. As we've said, it's easy to write, "Goal: $3 million" on the board; it's a lot harder to know if the business has the chops to get there.

Transparency and communication are key components of success. By being transparent and open, businesses can build trust and foster strong relationships with both their employees and customers. One way to achieve transparency is by documenting and communicating the business's vision, mission, strategy, performance, SOPs, and culture both internally and externally.

Having a published vision and mission is an essential first step for any successful business. A well-defined vision and mission statement help to clarify what the business stands for, what it aims to achieve, and how it plans to get there. These statements act as a guidepost for decision making and help to keep everyone aligned with the company's goals and objectives.

To execute its mission and meet shareholder profit- and value-growth goals, a business must use a written strategy. A sound strategy defines how the business plans to achieve its goals and lays out a road map for success. Senior leadership must manage the business in line with the strategic plan, ensuring that everyone is working toward the same objectives and that the company is making progress toward its goals.

> **A well-defined vision and mission statement help to clarify what the business stands for, what it aims to achieve, and how it plans to get there.**

Senior leadership must also analyze and consider strategic capacity in all planning and execution projects. Strategic capacity refers to a business's ability to execute its strategy successfully. This includes having the necessary resources, cash, skills, and knowledge to carry out the plan. By considering strategic capacity in all planning and execution projects, businesses can anticipate potential roadblocks and take steps to mitigate them.

Finally, successful businesses actively and continuously use an execution leadership system to deploy their strategy. An execution system is a set of processes and tools that help translate the strategic plan into actionable steps, growth-driving OKRs. A well-defined execution leadership system ensures that the business is making progress toward their goals and that everyone is aligned with and accountable to the strategic plan.

By being transparent and communicating their vision, mission, strategy, performance, SOPs, and culture both internally and externally, businesses build trust and foster strong relationships with their employees and customers.

STRATEGIC CULTURE

Objective: The business culture helps deliver the vision, mission, and strategy.

No matter how strong your strategic plan is, its efficacy will be held back by members of your team if they don't share the proper culture. When it comes down to it, the people implementing the plan are the ones that make all the difference.

Peter Drucker says it best: Culture eats strategy for breakfast. This doesn't mean that strategic planning is unimportant. It does, however, underscore that it's people who execute plans, and if you have a workforce that's excited to come to work every day, it makes a huge difference. So why the term strategic culture? Because great culture doesn't happen by accident. Great culture is the result of hard work and focus and needs to be nurtured. Strategic culture is created purposefully and promotes successful strategic execution. Happy, engaged people make natural strategic doers.

Here are several hallmarks of a strategic culture, many of which are found in other OKRs that feed strategic culture (you know, it's that gears-in-the-engine thing again). These need to be in place or else created and implemented:

- Business Story: Every employee knows the business's story, where it's going, and their role in getting it there.

- Transparency: The more the business shares key information internally and externally, the better.

- Discussion: Hand in glove with transparency, well-run businesses actively promote discussion of goals, strategy, tactics, and key metrics.

- One Number: Every employee can define success in the job using one number. Metrics are everywhere, they are tracked and discussed, and the business lives its numbers, including those with and those without dollar signs.

- Celebrating Mistakes: There's no good news or bad news, only data; by celebrating mistakes, senior leadership makes it clear that it's OK to miss so long as the reasons for the miss are documented, discussed, and used to make better decisions going forward.

- Defined Guiding Principles (a.k.a. Core Values): These should be meaningful and tied to the vision and mission (not just a list of happy words or table ante notions like trust and integrity). Guiding principles are brought to life through behavior, and the entire team—senior leaders, employees, and contractors—should manifest these principles through their work.

- Innovation is sought, promoted, celebrated, and harnessed as intellectual property and a competitive asset.

Most businesses say they have a culture, and most say they have core values. We hear this latter term get thrown around a lot. We should think about core values as guiding principles. The US Constitution is a document of basic principles. It does not say, "Have honesty and integrity because those are table ante." If a client says that honesty and integrity are their core values, have they told us anything we didn't expect? We want values that align and support the vision, mission, and strategy of the business. We want the employees to feel the same and take ownership of the values. A great example of ownership culture is the story about JFK and the janitor:

During a visit to the NASA space center in 1962, President John F. Kennedy noticed a janitor carrying a broom. He interrupted his tour, walked over to the man, and said, "Hi, I'm Jack Kennedy. What are you doing?"

"Well, Mr. President," the janitor responded, "I'm helping put a man on the moon."

To most people, this janitor was just cleaning the building. But in the more mythic, larger story unfolding around him, he was helping to make history.[30]

Strategic culture starts at the top. Too often we see an idea of culture among the senior leadership and a totally different idea of culture in the warehouse. As an advisor, it is important to call out the leadership and tell them that you should be seeing the guiding principles at every level of the business. See it in the behavior. See it in the language. Not an aspirational goal, a common behavior. Something everyone believes in and does that is more than just words on a wall.

It is important to think about what a strong culture looks like in today's economy with today's makeup of the workforce. Not every culture fits every business. But as advisors, we cannot just rubber stamp and say this is a good culture. Culture is created. It is a process based on common parameters and the needs of the individuals and of the organization. And it is the leader's responsibility to create and foster strategic culture.

You know when a business has a strategic culture when you walk through the door, call the customer support line, place an order, or take a delivery. Businesses who create and maintain strategic culture outperform because they are positive places to work and positive businesses to buy from. Full stop.

PEOPLE: HIRING AND TRAINING

Objective: There is a documented and effective process to hire, onboard, and train people that has a proven record of creating productive and loyal contributors to the business's success.

---

30   John Nemo, "What a NASA Janitor Can Teach Us about Living a Bigger Life," Business Journals, December 23, 2014, https://www.bizjournals.com/bizjournals/how-to/growth-strategies/2014/12/what-a-nasa-janitor-can-teach-us.html.

Having a strategic culture is an asset when attracting talent. As discussed in chapter 5, compensation and benefits at or above industry norms drive loyalty. Including performance-based incentives serves to intensify the loyalty of a business's most productive workers. But it is more than that. When it comes to hiring and training, there must be a written process to attract employees who will become productive and loyal as quickly as possible.

The business must have, or be willing to create, a documented and proven process to identify and hire employees and contractors. We exist in a gig economy, and contractors need to be included here. Our clients need to attract talent. So we as advisors need to help our clients build a talent bench. If there is someone whom leadership believes should be part of the business, then they should be. Sometimes even if there is no open position.[31] We should not allow a CEO to say, "I love that person. They would be great for the company, and I wish we could hire them, but we don't have an opening." If that person would be a great addition to the company, figure it out. Don't wait for an opening. Get the right people into the business. Build a culture on the people who fit, not the people you have—we are looking forward, not backward. Devote the same amount of time and energy to hiring the people and making the company compelling as is done with marketing and sales.

> **Devote the same amount of time and energy to hiring the people and making the company compelling as is done with marketing and sales.**

---

31   This seems contrary to not paying for excess capacity. The difference is that "right people" are hard to find; here, we are making a strategic decision to secure an individual. This contrasts with paying for capacity without the need or a plan to generate ROI.

LARGE MARKET SIZE

Objective: The market supports significant growth of the business including one or more of the following: geographic opportunities, diversifying revenues from current customers, noncannibalizing new sales, and strategic acquisitions.

Obviously if you are going to grow the business, it needs to grow into something. The business needs to have documented the size of the market that can be reached by the business in its current form. Can the business defend (with data) *three* reasons why the current market allows profitable growth in the future? Is there a significant market into which to grow? If not, the strategic growth project plan needs to identify alternatives—new markets, new products, and new services.

UNIQUE PRODUCTS/SERVICES

Objective: The products and/or services have unique characteristics that allow you to sell on value not price.

Growing profits also benefits from having products or services that have unique characteristics, allowing your client to sell on value not price and attract customers. Unique products are protected from commodity pricing and can sell on value. Plus, differentiated products often fetch a premium and win in head-to-head competition against other options. Differentiation can be driven by the customer's why, so if the features and functionality are the same, you can differentiate with guarantees, better delivery, loyalty programs, etc.

As discussed in chapter 5, too often there can be a race to the bottom. This occurred in the railroad industry in the late nineteenth century before JP Morgan reorganized the industry, and it occurred among gun manufacturers more recently. Specifically, the big makers Winchester and Remington went from making high-quality products to junk. Weak leadership competes on price, trying to undercut each other. Remington no longer exists. Winchester is a mess. The opposite happened in the automotive industry after foreign manufacturers entered the US market in force during the '70s and '80s. The foreign makers, especially the Japanese, delivered a product that at first delivered more reliability for a lower cost and over time evolved to deliver reliability, power, and comfort at similar cost to US makers, and in the same time period, the Europeans introduced reliable luxury machines that sold on value rather than price.

Product differentiation is key to supporting price. Your client must stay firm and communicate value. This is as true for drywall screws as it is for legal services. Strategic culture can contribute. Our role is ideally to help clients sell on value, not on price. If they don't, they risk being commoditized.

SCALABLE MARKETING PROCESS

Objective: The business can produce leads in a proven and systematic way, ensuring adequate potential customers at each stage of the buyer's journey.

With the Dimension 1 touchstone of scalable sales process in place, growing profits and value requires us to find new customers, and this is the province of marketing. Marketing as we discuss it here doesn't mean brand equity or another soft objective. Marketing here considers the ability to produce leads in a proven and systematic way, ensuring adequate potential customers at each stage of the buyer's journey. Marketing generates leads; leads feed sales. Leads need to be defined and qualified, and marketing should be held accountable to revenues just like sales is. A well-run business understands the value of every lead and when it can expect a pool of leads to convert into cash.

A clear and well-documented marketing plan is a must. A business should use a written marketing plan and process that track marketing performance metrics and are accountable for business revenue targets.

This all gets tied together as KPIs in the flash report (discussed in chapter 9). If we know that every marketing qualified lead is worth $124 in thirty-two days, we know how many of these leads are needed to hit a revenue goal.

A plan is not enough, though, and routine engagements in specific and organized actions are needed to interest potential customers. Such documented objectives must be SMART—Specific, Measurable, Ambitious, Realistic, and Timely—and include priorities, milestones, and targets. But we have to also be careful that our clients are ready to move into marketing. They may want to jump ahead. How many times have you heard clients assure you that their marketing program will solve all their problems? Marketing pouring leads into an ineffective sales process is like pouring water on cement: It won't penetrate far. Focusing first on Dimension 1's sales OKR before focusing on this marketing OKR maximizes ROI. It is our job as advisors to guide them and understand when the time is right for adding marketing to sales—the data will tell us.

FINANCIAL: BUDGET, FORECASTS, ACTUALS

Objective: The business manages finances using a budget and forecasts and has a documented history of actual financial performance at or above forecast.

Let's pause for a second and revisit the notion of a budget. Think of how folks discuss the budget. Often people see it as a license to spend money. That's lazy thinking. And crazy as it sounds, in many businesses if you don't spend what's in your budget, you lose it for the next year, so you have to spend, right? This can lead to frivolous spending and waste. A budget is an allocation of resources; a forecast figures out where the business is going. The client needs to "think and do" strategically by combining budget, forecasts, and tracking actual performance.

In Dimension 1 the OKR was to create and document strong financial reporting processes, including the implementation of flash reports. Dimension 2 growth is expensive since growth burns cash, often at an alarming rate. In Dimension 2 you are going to focus on budgets and forecasting: You need to have a sharp eye on the impact that growth will have on cash flow.

Growing revenues does not solve cash crunches. To the contrary, it is possible to grow a business to death. How do I know? There is a formula made popular by *Harvard Business Review* through which one can calculate the growth rate that a business can afford.[32] Simply put, ignore this rate and the business will inevitably run out of cash. Moreover, if your client has an eye on Dimension 3, having a record of using budgets, forecasting results, and tracking actuals against results is a surefire way to create confidence in future performance. And say it with me: Confidence in future results drives transferable value.

Confidence in future results drives transferable value.

Too often, businesses in the middle market (especially under $10 million) do not have good financial accounting and reporting discipline. They may have outsourced their bookkeeping. They look at the books maybe monthly, although they watch cash account balances, AP, and AR more closely.

We need to bring it all together into a process that has periodic budgets, forecasts future revenues and expenses, and tracks the relationship between the two. These numbers become the key perfor-

---

32 Neil Churchill and John Mullins, "How Fast Can Your Company Afford to Grow?" *Harvard Business Review*, May 2001, https://hbr.org/2001/05/how-fast-can-your-company-afford-to-grow.

mance indicators tracking weekly how the business is doing and predicts how it will do. These are woven into the flash report so that they are communicated and discussed.

INNOVATION CREATES A COMPETITIVE ADVANTAGE

Objective: The business understands the value of innovation and has a proven and systematic way to drive and capture innovation from employees, vendors, customers, and the market at all levels and for every area of the business.

Like "strategy" and "marketing," innovation is an ill-defined slippery eel of a term. It won't surprise you that embedding innovation in our culture and using it as a guiding principle can make a profound contribution to growth. Lots of businesses have a suggestion box and have a history of implementing good ideas. But is innovation sought, promoted, and celebrated? Promoting and rewarding innovation is key to growth; it's a hallmark of strategic culture. And protecting innovation as intellectual property is critical as well, linking us with Dimension 3.

As we approach Dimension 3, remember that we started the design conversation discussing predictable profits and cash flow. We then moved into leveraging predictable profits and cash flow as a launchpad for growth, creating predictable growth. We are now going to shift into predictable transferable value, to having high confidence in the price the business can generate at the deal table. Dimension 3 is about preparing the business so that it has a high likelihood of success executing one of two options: being able to successfully complete M&A or successfully transfer ownership and control by whatever path suits the shareholders.

RECAP

Predictable, profitable growth creates a business that generates a high ROI from its investments in growth. When we say ROI, we mean not only in terms of generating net new revenues and potentially net new transferable value, but ROI in that for every dollar we spend, we are going to get more than one dollar back. Dimension 2 builds on Dimension 1 to track and predict cash and growth.

As in each of the dimensions, Dimension 2 has eight high-priority OKRs. While in Dimension 1 we had a lot of internal focus, in Dimension 2 we are blending internal and external forces, starting to look out at the market around us, asking, "Is there a market into which we can grow with our current products, services, and SOPs?" and "How do we compare to the competition?" Marketing is optimized to increase revenues from sales, and the marketing process is linked to the sales process. We also focus on product differentiation to increase margins and drive growth. Innovation is sought, promoted, and protected, in fact becoming part of strategic culture, embedding this OKR into the business's DNA. The culture rewards winning, and the business has high capacity through sixteen optimized growth drivers.

Author's note: at the time of this writing, ChatGPT was making big waves. We asked GPT4 to apply the Dimension 1 and 2 growth-driving objectives to Ridge Specialty Tooling, and here is the answer. Imagine advising—or owning—this business:

> Ridge Specialty Tooling is a well-structured and managed business that focuses on achieving its vision and mission through effective leadership and accountability. The business has a strong track record of achieving its objectives and exceeding industry norms in terms of gross and net margins.

The employees and contractors of Ridge Specialty Tooling understand their roles and how they contribute to the company's overall goals. This is because the company has well-defined metrics for individual and team success, which are aligned with the company's objectives.

The business has a solid understanding of its future revenue streams and can predict a significant portion of its revenue through contracts or other means. The company regularly prepares financial reports, including P&L, balance sheet, and cash flow reports, and flash reports that track key performance metrics.

Ridge Specialty Tooling has a documented sales process with a proven track record of success that is universally applied and scalable. The company also has strong, documented standard operating processes that ensure consistent delivery on promises made to customers.

The business regularly measures customer satisfaction and uses this information to manage and improve performance. The company is transparent in its communication of its vision, mission, strategy, performance, SOPs, and culture both internally and externally.

The business culture is focused on delivering the company's vision, mission, and strategy and has a strong process for hiring, onboarding, and training employees to ensure they become productive and loyal contributors to the company's success.

The market for Ridge Specialty Tooling supports significant growth opportunities, including geographic expansion, diversification of revenue streams, noncannibalizing new sales, and strategic acquisitions. The company's products and services have unique characteristics that allow it to sell on value, not price.

Ridge Specialty Tooling has a systematic way of generating leads, ensuring an adequate number of potential customers at each stage of the buyer's journey. The business manages its finances using budgets and forecasts and has a documented history of actual financial performance at or above forecast.

Finally, the company understands the value of innovation and has a proven process to drive and capture innovation from employees, vendors, customers, and the market at all levels and for every area of the business.

We couldn't wish Ridge better ourselves. Now let's look at connecting this incredible performance to equity value by moving into Dimension 3.

DIMENSION 3 OF BUSINESS GROWTH

Predictable Transferable Value

After reading this chapter, you will understand the eight OKRs that must be in place to move a business from its status quo to delivering predictable transferable value.

In the previous two chapters, we first focused on generating predictable profits and cash by focusing on internal issues: operational efficiencies, making sure we understand and maximize margin, the link between recurring revenues and customer satisfaction, having a good sales process—all using documented OKRs. We then moved into predictable growth with strategy, strategic culture, and embracing innovation plus scalable marketing to layer new leads on top of our sales process. Now we need to wrap the business up in a bow for the next owners.

The operational manual for the business needs to create high confidence so that any buyer knows they will be able to predictably generate revenue, profits, and growth. Telling the business story that includes highly credible numbers, documented growth in market share that outshines the competitors, a diverse revenue base, and a defensible market for future revenues indicates that the business knows how to do its thing. It can tell its story, and it can defend future income, coupled with a strong culture that supports the vision and mission.

Let's begin with why Dimension 3 is "predictable transferable value."[33] As we've discussed, the link between revenues and value is not automatic. But most of your clients think that it is. They mistakenly believe if they have doubled their revenue, they will have doubled their value. Cue the buzzer. In fact, you can grow a business and actually have a net negative impact on transferable value.

Just because your client wants to sell their business doesn't mean the business itself is an asset that someone else would want to own. Mergers and acquisitions are not available to most companies. Nineteen out of twenty companies cannot approach the M&A market as they are currently run. This is often because the current owner has an unrealistic expectation of value (ask any M&A banker) that has nothing to do with real transferable value. Keep in mind that transferable value is the amount a financial buyer will pay for the business after completing due diligence. As discussed in chapter 2, due diligence is the process of uncovering all the risks to future revenue and profit. In other words, transferable value is the value of the business minus the risk. Buyers invest in high-risk businesses all the time—they simply account for risk in the price they pay. High-risk businesses have lower transferable value; the nontransferable portion is held back and may be monetized at a later date by the new owners.

All businesses trade in a normalized range, for example from 2X earnings to 6X earnings. Where a business falls in this range is driven by risk. Increased risk decreases value; mitigating risk increases value. Our clients need to think of their businesses in the same terms as they think of public companies: as having a Price to Earnings (P/E) ratio. The same principles apply. To quote Growth Specialist Greg

---

33 Strategic and synergistic value are outside the scope of this book; we are going to describe value as value to a financial buyer.

Maddox, clients need to stop doing operator math and start doing owner math. What does he mean? That clients need to stop thinking about growing revenues from $1 million to $2 million. As owners, they need to start thinking about growing value from $2 million to $6 million by increasing their multiple from 2X to 6X.

Using due diligence as a tool, private equity (PE) identifies businesses that meet their risk tolerance and for whom they are confident they can neutralize these risks. For example, PE buys the business at 2X earnings, they boil the risks out of the business (using the very same OKRs as you'll deploy in using the three dimensions of business growth), and they sell the business at 6X. As a growth driver you understand the link between business processes and transferable value and are able to promise your client that not only will you help them grow profits, but you will also help them make the purposeful link between growing profits and growing value.

It starts by educating your client. The owner too often has an unrealistic notion of what the company is worth. They have a value in their mind, and then a buyer comes in with a much lower (and more realistic due to strategic capacity) price. The owner does not like the price and backs out of discussions. By educating clients about the value, we are giving them a more realistic idea of what to expect from M&A. This can be a very emotional discussion, but it can also provide an opportunity to educate our client about strategic capacity and how to improve growth capacity and value capacity thereby decreasing risk and increasing value.

A word of caution. Let's say you're introduced to a client who wants to sell their business in six months. Do you simply open your playbook to Dimension 3 and magically create maximized transferable value? No. Dimension 3 includes the OKRs required for an M&A or similar transaction, but unless the business is strong in Dimensions

1 and 2, it may not be attractive to the market. The most prevalent deal killers are:

- Senior Leadership: If the business cannot grow without the CEO, then pulling them out of the business will hurt or even kill it.

- Legal: Litigation, failure to comply with relevant regulations, and a compromised equity stack are the leading gremlins.

- Noncredible Financials: If a buyer starts to question the accuracy of the financial reports (not because they're a jerk, but because they find discrepancies), then they'll politely excuse themselves from further conversations.

Imagine suddenly needing to present a history of credible financial reports without having laid the groundwork of Dimensions 1 and 2. No reporting process, no flash reports, no budgets with forecasts and actuals. Due diligence would be a nightmare. And in all likelihood, it would fail.

High-value businesses have high strategic capacity. They are immortal as they will transcend the founder's career. If a business is not immortal, then its story ends when the founder leaves the business. This happens to a lot of businesses, and it is bad for employees, vendors, stakeholders, customers, and the communities in which they live. The founder needs to understand that the value in the business is not in the business as it is today, it is in the business as it will be tomorrow. The more confident the buyers are in a bright tomorrow (without the CEO), the more they will pay. The job of the architect and general contractor to this point has been to execute a redesign of the business so that it can produce predictable cash and growth. Layering on predictable value is supported by this earlier work and now becomes the strategic goal.

Dimension 3 is simple: What OKRs need to be in place to ensure the business can trade at the top end of the range of multiples? If we shoot for a high M&A multiple, generally speaking regardless of which of the exit paths that the CEO chooses, you will have maximized value for that path. In addition to M&A, these options include ESOP, management buyouts, and stock redemption plans, gifting, liquidation, and IPO.

Let's move into Dimension 3 and the eight growth-driving objectives that must be reached to drive predictable transferable value.

	GROWTH DRIVER	BEST PRACTICE	OBJECTIVES
1	Strategic: Business Story	You have a document anyone could read and get a complete understanding of your business.	You have documented your business industry, niche, history (in words and financial results), organization, and locations that would allow an outsider to quickly gain a clear understanding of what your business does, how it does it, and the business's promise to the market.
2	Financial: Accurate and Credible Financial Reports	Your business financial reports and filings are accurate.	Your business's financial reports are routinely reviewed by independent outside experts, which confirms your financial performance and tax compliance, and your business could successfully complete an audit, quality of earnings, M&A due diligence, or similar outside inspection.
3	Legal: IP, Contracts, Governance, and Litigation	Your legal house is in order.	You have up-to-date legal documentation for key business areas including IP, employees, contractors and vendors, and corporate governance, and there is no litigation involving the business.
4	High Growth Compared to Market	Your business is growing faster than its competitors.	You document and discuss your business growth compared to your past performance, to your competitors, and to the market, and you can defend growth projections looking into the future.

5	Large Market Share	Your business owns the highest percentage of the available market relative to its competitors.	Your business owns the highest percentage of the available market relative to its competitors, and you maintain data on the market, this business's share, and the relative share of key competitors.
6	Broad Customer Base	Your business generates revenue from a large number of customers.	Your business generates revenue from a large number of customers, and no more than 20% of revenues come from your largest customer.
7	Defensible Market	You can defend your market and future revenues from new competitors.	You can defend your market and future revenues from new competitors using legal barriers, financial barriers, SOPs, or other barriers.
8	Strong Brand	Your brand is a valuable competitive tool.	Your brand is a valuable competitive tool that supports your vision, mission, and strategic execution.

STRATEGIC: BUSINESS STORY

Objective: The business has documented the business industry, niche, history (in words and financial results), organization, and locations that would allow an outsider to quickly gain a clear understanding of what your business does, how it does it, and the business's promise to the market.

The business needs to be able to tell its story. It's logical: If the business cannot tell its own story internally and to the world, how will it explain to the market (customers and potential acquirers) how it does what it does? If it cannot tell its own story, why should anyone pay attention to this business? Why should they invest their time and money in what it does?

In addition to the business's origin story, the work you've completed in Dimensions 1 and 2 can be threaded together into a narrative. Historic flash reports tell a story, especially when coupled with historic P&Ls, balance sheets, and cash reports. The sales and marketing processes and plans tell a story. The guiding principles and strategic culture tell a story. The goal is to have an operating manual for the business with the narrative and financial details that prove that the operating manual works and will continue to work going into the future.

FINANCIAL: ACCURATE AND CREDIBLE FINANCIAL REPORTS

Objective: Your client's business's financial reports are routinely reviewed by independent outside experts, which confirms their financial performance and tax compliance, and the business could successfully complete an audit, quality of earnings, M&A due diligence, or similar outside inspection.

As we indicated, financial reports must be credible. It's a bridge that can't be burned. You get issued credit on trust when first doing business with someone. That's credit that can be burned if promise and reality don't line up. It's critical, and business owners muck this up routinely. They will get to the deal table, present financials, and we come to find out through due diligence that the numbers are wrong. Fiasco. Suddenly the buyer is asking, "If the numbers are wrong, what else is?" The financial story needs to tie every dollar of revenue to a customer and every expense to a legitimate business purpose.

> **The financial story needs to tie every dollar of revenue to a customer and every expense to a legitimate business purpose.**

Legitimate business purpose means that the owner has for at least three years taken compensation and benefits in line with industry norms. In other words, they have not used the business to fund their lifestyle. We touched on this point earlier: As a general rule, business owners hate taxes (at some level, don't we all?) and view profits as a target for the tax man. This attitude naturally leads them to actually try and minimize profits. Some of this spending is for the good—business revenues funding real estate acquisition, advantage taken of tax incentives promoting the purchase of durable equipment, etc. Unfortunately some also goes into personal real estate and questionable business expenses like boats and vacations. The client views paying the minimum tax required by law as the goal. But you need to expect that prior tax obligations will come up in seller's reps and warranties, and the business's historic tax returns will need to be defensible at the deal table.

And here's the catch-22: The dubious strategies used to avoid taxes depress profits. For most (but not all) industries, the trading multiple is applied to EBITDA (earnings before interest, taxes, depreciation, and amortization). By depressing EBITDA, the shareholders are depressing transferable value. A dollar of tax avoidance today is $6 of value tomorrow. We're not going to get into valuation add-backs here; suffice it to say that the best practice is to arrive at the deal table with a clean story.

There has been a growing standard practice of buyers sending accountants into the target business to perform a quality of earnings analysis. Consider why they do this. The buyer is trying to gain confidence in historic numbers and in the sales projections for the future. If this exercise is valuable for the buyer, why wouldn't it be valuable for the seller? What will your client's world look like if they run the business every day in a way that is aligned with a quality of earnings checklist? Implementing the three dimensions of business growth accomplishes this and a whole lot more.

For this reason, businesses should conduct a self-audit before moving toward an M&A or other transaction. You'll help identify issues ahead of time and help your client prepare. What also sometimes happens, and can blow up a potential deal, is lax compliance with state/local income and sales tax reporting. Even if not consciously, many businesses may not be in total compliance. This is often not on purpose as they do not even realize taxes are owed in a state in which they may only have one or two customers. Plenty of states take a broad view of economic nexus, and while the business does not think twice about it, count on it to come up during due diligence. The buyer may view bringing the business into tax compliance as a risk and escrow some amount of the price until the risk is mitigated.

The work done building financial reporting tools for understanding and leading the business in Dimension 1 and Dimension 2 will have laid the groundwork for Dimension 3. To this, add the metrics from marketing that explain the value of qualified leads and the data from sales detailing the buying history of the customer base, and you have the core ingredients for whistling through a quality of earnings review, an audit, and due diligence. The work to strengthen the gears in the business engine is moving the business in all three dimensions. It's a beautiful thing.

LEGAL: IP, CONTRACTS, GOVERNANCE, AND LITIGATION

Objective: The business has up-to-date legal documentation for key business areas including IP, employees, contractors and vendors, and corporate governance, and there is no litigation involving the business.

OK, this is a lot to unpack. And also not easy to nail. The earlier you start working with your client on this objective the better. Please read the objective again. Now imagine the time it will take, and the low level of excitement most clients will have to tackle it, and you can see you'll need to lay the groundwork for this early on.

Talk with any M&A pro and they'll tell you that legal docs rank right up there with financial as both a headache and stressor for the client. One piece of advice: If you're starting a long-term engagement, consider putting this objective on the CEO's radar early. Convincing them to improve financial reporting and implementing flash reports makes sense; getting them to gather board minutes and corporate contracts is an order of magnitude more difficult. Do not let the client kick this can too far down the road. You never know when an unsolicited M&A offer may come in or when the business could pounce on a strategic opportunity requiring outside capital. A messy legal house will muck things up quickly.

> **If you're starting a long-term engagement, consider putting this objective on the CEO's radar early.**

The legal side, if not viewed carefully, can blow up a deal. Here's a real-world example: A business had contracts with two major vendors who supplied it with most of its materials. In the supply contracts, each vendor could terminate the contract if there was a change in the buyer's ownership. When they notified the vendors of the pending sale, you guessed it, both vendors terminated. This blew up the deal because the vendors were strategic to the business. You and your client need to have the right lawyers on board early so there is awareness of small details in contracts that do not become landmines when it comes time to sell.

One more thing: Most businesses have an attorney. These may be attorneys the business has had for twenty years. They are trusted and valued. And while competent counsel on corporate matters, most of those attorneys have never done a transaction. A good transaction attorney is essential and worth their fee. The expense may initially cause heartburn, but the efficiency and knowledge that the right attorney brings is worth it. Advise your client on the need to bring in specialized legal counsel in two areas: tax planning and M&A prep. Expensive, but the ROI from both is immense (if not immediate) and generally pays for itself through added value in the transaction.

HIGH GROWTH COMPARED TO MARKET

Objective: The business documents and discusses growth compared to past performance, to competitors, and to the market and can defend growth projections looking into the future.

Let's talk about the client's growth in the context of the market. To earn a top multiple, the business must be growing in relation to its past, in relation to its peers, and in relation to the market. Look at the work done to date: Getting a high score in this area should be a chip shot. There are several Dimension 1 and 2 objectives that feed this Dimension 3 OKR. Financial reports, flash reports, and the data from competitive monitoring all feed success here. Your client must be able to document growing revenues and profits, track financial performance against the market (and key competitors), and articulate and defend three or more reasons why it will continue to grow compared to those competitors and the market. If you're looking for supporting data, consult with a valuator like a CVA; they can help gather this data.

LARGE MARKET SHARE

Objective: The business has defined their market and niche and has data showing they have a dominant market share versus key competitors.

Having a dominant market share demonstrates the ability to outperform competitors, and that can increase the multiple by increasing buyer confidence. If you are not already crushing the competition, but you can show a plan to gain market share or to become the dominant market player, you create buyer confidence. This goes back to whether we have defined our niche and a well-presented business story.

Creating buyer confidence increases when the business owns the highest percentage of the available market relative to its competitors. This confidence grows if the business can document the size of the market and its market share and identify the key competitors (both real and perceived). Further data on the market, this business's share, and the relative share of key competitors helps clearly communicate why the business will retain market position or how it will attain a dominant market position. Such a business can articulate and defend its place in the world.

BROAD CUSTOMER BASE

Objective: The business generates revenue from a large number of customers, with no more that 20 percent of revenues coming from the largest customer.

Most business owners who generate revenue from a small number of customers cannot sleep at night. We'll leave government contractors to the side for now because they only have one customer. We want customers in different stages of evolution: new customers and established customers. Every customer has a life cycle, and we want to document that. The business should be able to describe and defend three or more reasons for future diversification of revenue streams.

This is another example of a Dimension 3 objective that needs to feature in the strategic growth project plan from the earlier dimensions. This objective is a strategic imperative because concentrating revenues in a few customers creates existential risk to cash flow and growth. Bring this objective up early and maintain focus all throughout your engagement. Businesses are, generally speaking, better playing Moneyball than swinging for the fences. [34]

DEFENSIBLE MARKET

Objective: The business can defend its market and future revenues from new competitors using legal barriers, financial barriers, SOPs, or other barriers.

Is there a moat around your client's business? Can they defend their market and future revenues? Having a moat creates confidence in future earnings, and confidence—say it with me—drives high multiples. What are examples of defenses? A high cost to enter the market (financial barrier), intellectual property such as patents or proprietary SOPs, even a dominant brand (I know, technically also IP but worth calling out). These need to be documented and added to the business story.

STRONG BRAND

Objective: The brand is a valuable competitive tool that supports the business's vision, mission, and strategic execution.

Brand is a term that gets bandied about like many others. Like "strategy," it is a word that is often used but rarely understood and harnessed to the growth engine. Let's get practical. A strong brand is valuable intellectual property that can be sold separately from ongoing operations. A strong brand is also a competitive advantage.

> **Brand is arguably the outward manifestation of strategic culture.**

---

34   *Moneyball* is a book by Michael Lewis and a terrific 2011 film starring Brad Pitt based on the Oakland A's 2002 season in which they built a winning team by signing many players who could hit singles rather than a few players who could hit home runs. The strategy worked, and they won more games in a row than any team in Major League Baseball history.

Brand is arguably the outward manifestation of strategic culture. So seen through the idea of gears in the business engine, brand connects to marketing in terms of brand values. Like guiding principles provide promises to stakeholders, brand value can offer promises to the market. A strong brand supports customer loyalty. Brand is a growth driver, and it can also put a golden thumb on the value scale.

What should you help your client do? They need to quantify the brand as a valuable competitive tool that supports the business's vision, mission, and strategic execution. Is this an objective that can be reached quickly? It depends on the data your client keeps. The longer the client has been working on their brand as a strategic asset, the better. Metrics from recurring revenues and customer satisfaction bolster this story.

BONUS: STRENGTH OF THE M&A MARKET

There's a bonus growth-driving objective: time to market. This can be considered Dimension 4 in relation to the three dimensions of business growth. In general, the M&A market follows the same ten-year peak-and-valley cycles as the general economy.[35] In 2021, we were in a booming M&A market that delivered two results: businesses that normally could not have gone to market successfully did and well-run businesses earned multiples above traditional norms. Why is this important? Because you can educate your client about these trends and potentially time the potential business transfer with a boom cycle.

No one has a crystal ball, but if trends hold, if past performance is a predictor of future events, you can help your client at least aim

---

35   Robert Slee, *Private Capital Markets: Valuation, Capitalization, and Transfer of Private Business Interests* (Hoboken, NJ: Wiley, 2011).

at having the option to sell the business at the top of the market or to prepare the business to sell in a down market. Even in a down market, owners monetize value. The difference is that the things you can sweep under the rug in a go-go market become a dead elephant in the room when the market is down. Acknowledging the importance of time as Dimension 4 reinforces the process of the three dimensions to constantly reviewing the business and reengineering and pivoting to increase value. As many advisors know, it takes a long time to build an "overnight success."

RECAP

Every industry has a normalized great trading range. Company-specific risk determines the multiple of revenues available in a deal. Low-risk businesses get a high multiple. Businesses with high strategic capacity present low-risk profiles. This is what Dimension 3 is about—creating high confidence in your client's ability to predictably generate growing revenue and profit going into the future. Confidence comes from a history and defensible projections of predictable cash flow and pre-dictable profitable growth. These need to be woven into the business story credibly in words and numbers. As a bonus, time to market is a strategic consideration that impacts transferability and value.

SPRINTS AND WATERFALLS

Executing the Strategic Growth Project Plan

After reading this chapter, you will understand the importance of transparency and of setting a meeting rhythm with accountability. After reading this chapter you will understand how to unpack and prioritize the growth-drive OKRs in a waterfall composed of sprints assigned to each senior leader with success metrics.

In this chapter, we begin to lay out the execution phase of the growth-drive action cycle by guiding you on how to build the strategic growth project plan. Included in this chapter is an example of the Gantt chart and a discussion of the benefits associated with it. We will also discuss how to lead sprints, which gets into deploying the execution leadership system described in chapter 10.

THE IMPORTANCE OF EXECUTION

Execution is currently a hot topic. The conference board recently surveyed CEOs and revealed that those CEOs were so concerned about strategy execution they rated it as their number one challenge. What is revealing when you look at that survey is that a staggering 60 percent of strategies are not successfully executed and implemented. This execution gap is often due to either one or both of the following:

a lack of communication and/or a lack of accountability. Both can prove to be a difficult but fixable challenge to CEOs executing the strategic growth project plan. This gives us a great opportunity as advisors to help our clients and guide them through the execution phase. We can facilitate and help them navigate the process to achieve a greater success rate than that dismal 60 percent.

In almost every business, people's biggest complaint is a lack of communication. They don't know what is going on in the organization. According to research from Franklin Covey, only 37 percent of employees surveyed[36] said they have a clear understanding of what their organization is trying to achieve, and only one in seven could name even one of the business's most important goals. Furthermore, 81 percent of those surveyed said they were not held accountable for regular progress.

> **In almost every business, people's biggest complaint is a lack of communication.**

If you applied those statistics to a football team, it would mean that only seven of eleven players knew what they were supposed to do, and of the eleven there are nine for whom the coaches aren't even keeping score. The best news is that we are able to influence and change those statistics through the execution process.

When you look at the management team, part of the problem—and probably a major issue—is likely the lack of accountability. We define accountability here as doing what you say you are going to do. Often, the management teams promise and do not deliver. That is exactly the reason why we advise and encourage you to start your engagement with a strategic capacity analysis that includes participation by the entire senior leadership team. Lack of accountability is a major

36   Jim Harter, *The State of the American Workplace 2017*, Gallup, February 7, 2017, https://www.gallup.com/workplace/237390/state-american-workplace-report-2017.aspx.

aspect of the dysfunction of the team. That lack of communication and lack of accountability causes this execution gap, which results in 60 percent of projects or plans not getting executed properly.

Our role as advisors through execution is to take a business from its (dysfunctional) status quo into alignment. In a workshop meeting with leaders, try asking them to close their eyes, put a hand up in the air, and point to south-southeast. Then ask them to open their eyes. The result? Many hands are pointing in different directions. That's a great segue into asking if that is happening in their business. More importantly, ask them what they are going to do about it. What does closing the execution gap look like? What are the benefits of closing the gap if they work on it? There are many benefits, with the most important being improved communication among the management team. Then encourage them to cascade that communication down to the rest of their employees.

INTRODUCING THE PROJECT PLAN

Writing the strategic growth project plan should begin with the client integrating their vision and mission into the plan. Integrating means not simply listing at the beginning but constantly asking if the project will help execute the mission. This is followed by evidencing commitment to the goal:

- Goal: Where do they want to go?

- Implication: What will happen if they don't get there?

- Time: When must the goal be reached?

- Budget: What people and resources are available to execute the plan?

- Accountability: Who is responsible for success and to whom?

Success is driven by alignment and transparency. The CEO needs to clearly define the growth goal. The senior team must be aligned with the goal and be "all in" for the work that must be done to reach it. Senior leaders in turn must communicate the goal, sprints, and success metrics to their teams, highlighting the collaboration needed among the various teams. Every team member must be aware and involved.

Executing strategy requires a strategic culture. Strategic culture is evident in senior leadership meetings. If senior leaders routinely gather to discuss the business, build relationships, and break down barriers, this sends a very powerful signal to the rest of the organization. In fact every member of the business should gather regularly in well-structured meetings, through which the execution gap begins to close.

As the advisor you will guide senior leaders to push transparency about goals and performance "down onto the shop floor," helping every employee and contractor understand what is going on and what they need to do. In addition, your work with the management team increases collaboration and gets them to hold each other accountable. This almost unavoidably drives the business forward.

Sometimes there's a misnomer of what accountability is for people on a team. It has to get us to where we want as a business or move to the consequence of not doing. It goes back to the *Why*. Teach the team to talk about *why* they didn't reach a key result or missed a KPI. We want to examine and openly, candidly discuss the reasons *why* they didn't achieve something. It's not about blame. It is not about failing. It is about learning from failure. In a sense, the path to success requires being comfortable with failure. Clients need to be comfortable with failure because there is actually no such thing as failure, only learning. That attitude, that paradigm, is exciting. It's a growth mindset.

At regular intervals you will review progress on the project with the CEO and senior leadership. You will list the work completed, establish employees' working history, track wins and challenges, and begin to look forward. This step includes listing sprints (discussed in more detail in the following pages), which are sequential, regular, and repeatable work cycles. You will help the CEO hold senior leaders accountable, giving credit for wins and accountability for misses. You will discuss with your client what the end looks like, explaining that each sprint builds to the next and hitting completion dates is critical to building momentum and maintaining execution rhythm.

You may include checklists to support executing the plan, making sure that every employee and contractor understands their role in relation to the goals of the company. Linking objectives and people with target scores for each growth-driving objective and key result will clarify the progress of the company in relation to the goal.

GANTT CHARTS: THE BLUEPRINT

The Strategic Growth Project Plan's Gantt Chart is a blueprint for execution, something that we can use to help guide our clients. We have talked about data, OKRs, prediction, and in the following chapter, flash reports and KPIs. We have talked about priorities. Here we introduce Gantt charts, which will serve as a foundation of executing the growth project by helping establish a rhythm of accountabilities discussed in client meetings.

So why is the Gantt chart important? It is a method to communicate and keep everybody focused on the fact that we are not eating the whole elephant in one bite. Think of the Gantt as a waterfall, where one OKR cascades into the next. This waterfall simply means that completing one phase (called a sprint) allows the business to move sequentially forward to the next. When we have run a complete analysis of the business, we have data on the business's alignment with defined OKRs. Now we are laying them out in a sequence in a project plan. In order to build from one OKR to the next, to start gaining momentum and moving in Dimension 1, assign objectives to the relevant senior leaders and list the attendant key results. Through execution you begin creating predictable profits and cash flow. You will have begun implementing the strategic growth project plan. There are online templates and resources accessible through the appendix.

Here's what a Gantt chart with a waterfall of sprints looks like:

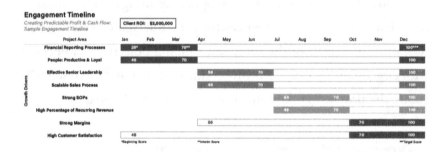

The waterfall model is a linear project management approach, where stakeholder requirements are gathered at the beginning of a sequential project plan. It is considered a waterfall model because each phase cascades into the next. It is also a thorough, structured methodology and one that has been around a long time because it works. Gantt charts are the preferred tool for working in a waterfall because using a Gantt chart allows you to map subtasks, dependencies, and each phase of the project.

The following are the elements of the Gantt chart:

- List of objectives and key results, which are time bound with start and end dates

- Total project timeline

- List of sprints to reach OKRs

- Also: consider in what areas we can lay groundwork *before* the start date so that we can hit the ground running when the time comes

- Link OKRs to delivering progress in the three dimensions

- Identify the one person who is accountable

As the owner is looking at this, he or she sees that each step is adding value toward their overall strategy of where they aspire to reach with the business.

Keep in mind how you are initially defining success. If you are using an analysis tool like the CLARITY Strategic Capacity Analysis, then you can easily use operational scores as success metrics, perhaps initially defining seventy as success; one hundred isn't necessary (or generally possible—there is no perfect business). We will work on getting close to 100 percent, and we will come back and shoot for "perfect" as the organization evolves. It's going to call for collaboration between teams. Teams are accountable for gears inside the business engine. Remember: None of these sprints exists in a vacuum. They all exist as part of the whole, and each will have an impact on the whole.

Our differentiator as growth drivers is access to tools that link achieving OKRs to the value of the business. Reaching growth-driving objectives in Dimensions 1 and 2 builds growth capacity; doing the same in Dimension 3 builds value capacity. From our very first conversation, from our first work with the senior team during the analysis phase, we have taught them to think in terms of strategic capacity and the impact that strategic capacity has on profits and transferable value. Importantly, because we are building strategic capacity, we are linking the work they are doing to creating predictable profits and growth. And we are always discussing increased capacity on those terms as well as in terms of the transferable equity value of the business, which again is the ultimate measure of business success.

> **Importantly, because we are building strategic capacity, we are linking the work they are doing to creating predictable profits and growth.**

As we have stressed, part of our objective is to leave an indelible positive mark on the business, to leave the business better than we found it. We want to teach the business to manage by OKRs and drive this thinking into the DNA of the business. You are literally redesigning the business so that they run into the future using the OKRs and analyze-design-execute cycle you have introduced. This collaborative process is a significant part of the value we deliver.

SPRINTS

The three dimensions of business growth provide the information that will be converted into a Gantt chart. The work to implement key results is called sprints. Sprints have a long history of success in execution methodologies like Agile, initially used by software development teams. Achieving the OKR is the main focus of the business for that period—a week, month, quarter, etc. Often completing one sprint is a prerequisite to beginning the next. For example, the business needs to collect timely and accurate financial data if it wants to implement forecasts and track actuals. We look at the sprints, understand how they waterfall together and build on each other, and understand when senior leaders are going to be held accountable and where we are in a supporting role. The Gantt chart helps communicate goals and processes the relationship between sprints (therefore OKRs). Each sprint is assigned to one executive and has a success metric. The tempo we are going to build is to distribute these logically so that one can build on the previous sequentially and logically in order for us to distribute accountability across the senior team.

OKRs must by definition be time bound. Allow one to three months to reach the objective. The client sets the pace, but we are going to hold them accountable to a schedule, and we are going to try as much as possible to stay on task and time. When we have buy-in from the senior leadership team, buy-in that we have been building up through the analyze and design phases, it ensures that when it comes to executing, they are going to stay on time and on target.

While the senior team is a resource, it has a day job, and the members have time constraints as well. The business can't come off the tracks because we are executing a growth project. That would be absolutely counterproductive. When you are planning and designing sprints, you must account for each executive's day job. As they execute, they must be able to focus on their core accountabilities and on their additional strategic accountabilities as well. We are going to spread the responsibilities around the team, and we are going to distribute them over time. Remember, one person is ultimately accountable for reaching each objective. This does not mean that only one person works on the OKR; they will need to collaborate and delegate to their teams. Ultimately only one person will be accountable for success.

You are also going to track subtasks and dependencies at each phase of the project as it moves through its life cycle. But we also don't want to overplan our project. This may seem counterintuitive, but you'll in all likelihood need to adjust along the way. Things happen, and the landscape can change. The standard is not about perfection, it is about getting the project going, registering some early wins and making adjustments as needed. Remember: analyze-design-execute is a cycle, where each execute sprint is followed by a pause to run analysis. Did creating a better sales process create a bottleneck in production and delivery? Better to identify and confirm bottlenecks early, or in this case we might be hurting customer satisfaction and recurring revenues.

Here is where the growth goal and analyze are so important to design and execute. Because requirements are gathered at the beginning of this sequential project plan, you and your client will have total clarity about what needs to get done (sprints) to achieve the success they want (growth goal). Focusing on the waterfall, each phase cascades into the next step, and we build strength incrementally and sequentially. This strength can be used as links in a chain.

EXECUTION THROUGH RHYTHMS

When we look at the idea of greatness, consider this quote from Jim Collins: "It's about a matter of conscious choice and discipline." As discussed above, you need to set the rhythm of well-structured meetings to ensure open communication and accountability. In order to establish the meeting rhythms, the management team needs to make a conscious choice and have a disciplined thought process and a disciplined approach to meetings. When they do, those meetings become the heartbeat of the business. Gino Wickman, author of the book *Traction,*[37] calls the rhythm a pulse, the meeting pulse that is the organization's heartbeat. What does that heartbeat look like? What does the meeting rhythm look like? It looks like a cadence of meetings, a consistent series of meetings where a leadership team meets without fail, no excuses, but a set time on a set day to drive progress and solve issues and help people move in alignment and sync. We'll cover this in detail in chapter 10 about the execution leadership system.

---

37   Gino Wickman, *Traction: Get a Grip on Your Business.* (Dallas: BenBella Books, 2012).

Let's go back to this strategy: What we just described in great detail with great focus is a plan: analyze, design, execute, analyze, design, etc., always checking positive progress toward the goal. That is what the rhythm of meetings does. If we go back to the first chapter and the growth conversation, as advisors we take the time to get at whether the client is still emotionally committed because growth is a roller coaster. Commitment is answered by the why, and unless we begin by getting that why, and unless that why is written on the heart of the owner, and he or she transmits that through his or her leadership to the leadership team, it becomes difficult to move the flywheel.

An important point to note: It's about *who* before *what*. In *Scaling Up* Verne Harnish calls this "The Right People Doing the Right Things Right." For example, a bookkeeper is probably not going to make a capable CFO, and often a salesperson does not perform well as a sales manager. If you are looking to grow the organization, you need to have the best talent to execute the role. We may reach a juncture on the road where we have to determine whether someone can be coached to success or decide that the person doesn't have the skills, temperament, or ambition to deliver. This can lead to tough conversations, but the conversations are necessary. As we indicated previously, what got you here will not get you there. That applies both to the owner or CEO, as well as to their people. As advisors moving forward, it is a predictable issue that often crops up. Have you thought through how you are going to handle it when it does, without destroying relationships?

When we think in terms of the long-term health of the organization, consider professional development. If we want to have a strong culture, where our people are invested in the success of the enterprise and where they feel valued, we are going to want to make sure they feel like they are developing as a professional as well. The military does it routinely. As a reward for doing a great job, send the employee to get his or her MBA and pay for it—perhaps suggesting they do it as an online course over the next three years. There are great ways to bake the expertise into the organization and to build a long-term, stable employee base.

Side note: This question often comes up among advisors. Is it cash we start with, or do we start with people? It's who before what, but we also need to focus on whether we can get quick wins to get the momentum of the project going and sustain it through the early days. Quick wins—achieving success in the first few sprints for example— are critical to creating (and maintaining) momentum in the project.

Another note: Carefully design your waterfall, making sure that you are respecting the day jobs of the senior team. You are going to want their buy-in as you build the strategic growth project plan. The execution is tracked, planned, and designed—and tracked again, which shows us the impact of not delivering an OKR. We are going to delineate execution and flow and show graphically the buildup of these OKR waterfalls. It becomes a reference point for team meetings and for collaboration. Couple this with flash reports (discussed in chapter 9) and you have an organization that is healthy, strong, and growing.

Think about the execution flow in this way (through Dimension 1 OKRs):

1. Effective Senior Leadership: Get the head on straight

2. People: Productive and Loyal: Right people, right things, right

3. Financial Reporting Processes: Accurate recordkeeping, performance transparency, KPIs tracking progress

4. High Percentage of Recurring Revenues: Engage sales team to secure contracts or other reasons customers will come back

5. High Margins: Updated fin reporting creates confidence in margin analysis (must be sure before making the changes); if below industry standards, understand *why*—is it sales discounting, inefficient production, waste, etc.?

6. Scalable Sales Process: With recurring revenue project, and understanding of margin, can you update pricing, improve value proposition, create replicable sales machine, etc.?

7. Strong SOPs: Delivering sales on time and to spec. This will improve recurring revenue and sales process flows through to delivery, and if there is a lack of recurring revenue caused by poor operations, then move up the stack.

8. High Customer Satisfaction: Track, get bad news, identify bottlenecks. This helps lead to unique products/services, scalable marketing process, and innovation plus touchstone recurring revenue (which helps Dimension 2 forecasting).

Throughout this process, it is vital to remember one thing: All of this is only as good as the commitment from the CEO, that they buy into the process. Transparency, commitment, and accountability are essential. We can find success when we see the following:

- We have defined OKRs for the business (3DoG).

- These have been hammered into an SGPP waterfall.

- The sprints in the plan have individual accountability to a defined success metric by a certain date.

- Now we need to add a meeting rhythm.

- In our meetings we will use our flash report to track progress.

- Weekly meetings of senior leadership and of functional teams

- Quarterly meetings of senior leadership and their direct reports

- Annual meetings of senior leadership and their direct reports

- Goals, sprints, and flash report information are shared and discussed throughout the organization.

- Analyze, Design, Execute: Where did we start, where are we now, where are we going, how will we get there, and how are we doing?

RECAP

There is an execution gap fueled by a lack of communication and accountability. Establishing a rhythm of meetings closes this gap, driving alignment and results. The rhythm consists of a series of programmed and structured meetings with a central focus on establishing a ninety-day sprint of plan. Implementing the result is a change management issue. Be prepared for pushback. Persistent pushing of the flywheel produces huge time savings and breakthrough results.

When businesses knuckle down and do it, they have a proven track record of increasing gross revenues an average of 21.63 percent per year. That's powerful! This is how you create a revenue-generating machine with sustainable growth of 20 percent per year, year over year. CEOs committed to robust growth are fun and rewarding to work with. These are the people and businesses you'll want to identify and help. Because these are the women and men who know where they want to go, are committed to the journey, and are willing to invest time and treasure driving to their win. These are your ideal clients, those through whom you will build a thriving advisory business.

9

FLASH REPORTS AND KPIS

Data with Accountability and Collaboration

*After reading this chapter, you will understand using key
performance indicators (KPIs) to track execution as a
powerful tool that, through flash reports, creates growth,
collaboration, accountability, and transparency.*

In this chapter we will continue with the execute phase of the growth-drive action cycle by focusing on key performance indicators (KPIs) and flash reports. KPIs, unfortunately, is another one of those terms that, like the word *strategy*, gets used so much that it is in danger of losing meaning. For our purposes, we want to look at KPIs as a set of quantifiable measurements used to gauge a business's overall long-term performance. KPIs can be ratios or individual numbers, and they can, but do not need to, have a dollar sign in front of them. In fact many of the most important numbers in the business do not have a dollar sign attached. Basically KPIs are numbers we use to manage the business. We want to track KPIs on a routine basis as we help the client form the

> **KPIs score your progress toward the strategic goals and tell you how you are doing.**

healthy habit of using a one-page flash report as a tool to help transform their business. KPIs are captured in the flash report, which is the dashboard for managing the business. KPIs score your progress toward the strategic goals and tell you how you are doing. Tracking the data is important, but perhaps most important is making people accountable to the data. Your clients need to see and understand the value of flash reports and the transparency, accountability, and collaboration that come with them. If you do nothing else, help your client form the habit of preparing, sharing, and discussing a weekly flash report—have this indelible positive impact.

KEY PERFORMANCE INDICATORS (KPIs)

KPIs are tracked and used to manage the business by tracking performance. They help you to determine, *Where are we today? Where did we say we were going to be?* Throughout this book, we have inferred several important KPIs, such as operating cash flow. The Fractional CFOs among you might add cash flow ratio, cash over sales, and gross and net margin percentage by product and service. Other data in the business story is free cash flow by month, recurring revenue by percentage of customers, dollar revenue per customer, annual (and lifetime) value of a customer, and customer mix. These are just a few of the KPIs we can track, which are systemically connected to senior leadership.

"Systemically connected" refers to a situation where different parts of a system are interconnected or interdependent in a way that affects the functioning of the system as a whole. In other words, changes or disruptions in one part of the system can have ripple effects on other parts of the system. For example, in a business organization, different departments such as sales, marketing, and finance are systemically connected because they all play a role in the overall success of the business. A change in one department's strategy or performance can affect the performance of other departments and the overall success of the business. Overall, the concept of systemic connectivity is important in understanding how different parts of a system interact and influence each other and how changes in one part of the system can affect the system as a whole.

After you have started to collect and report the KPIs, and you have discussed what they mean, the client becomes more familiar with a strong versus weak KPI and what this indicates as far as an opportunity for improvement. Then we start to add benchmarks. Next to every KPI, there will always be a benchmark of what our goal is for a desired KPI. Management begins to not only collect the actual performance, but they are also looking at where they want to be. That automatically opens up the opportunity to talk about ways that you can improve the overall performance and value of the business. Now you are starting to talk about not only the performance, but you are also benchmarking it against where you need to be and what action needs to happen in order to achieve the goals of the business.

Here's an example. Let's use alignment with a key result as a KPI. In the recurring revenue growth-driving objective, one key result is "The business can predict 50 percent (good) to 80 percent (better) of future revenue through contracts or other means." OK, let's set 50 percent as our KPI. Now we are tracking revenue against a benchmark. And once you do the same thing with a KPI for a broad customer base, tracking the mix of new/developing/long-term customers, and for high customer satisfaction with a target net promoter score, you create a systemically connected set of KPIs measuring performance of gears in the business engine against numeric goals.

Remember that tracking performance against goals is a key component of the analyze phase of the growth-drive action cycle. Accountability for each KPI must rest with only one senior executive, and no one is allowed to pass the buck. But also always make sure we are tracking those that are relevant to the business. Not everything can fit on the one-page report; don't worry, with use, the right data will stay and interesting-but-extraneous data will fall off the report.

FLASH REPORTS

When talking about flash reports and dashboards, the objective is twofold. First, we want to help our clients manage their business in real time. But it is also an opportunity to grow your practice in various areas of consulting. You can use a flash report as a link to the day-to-day activities of your client and create a relationship that sets you up as a go-to person within the organization. The flash reports can really help build that relationship.

To start, a flash report is a management tool that provides a one-month trend and contains the current week and three prior weeks of financial information. It includes key performance indicators to identify areas of concern, issues for improvement, and monitoring the progress of current initiatives. Preferably, the report is on one page (8½ x 11).

> **To start, a flash report is a management tool that provides a one-month trend and contains the current week and three prior weeks of financial information.**

A dashboard is nothing more than an electronic flash report. The only issue about a dashboard is that it becomes another stumbling block if it takes more time to create and more time to maintain. Stumbling blocks can really hurt an engagement, and we want this to be as seamless as possible so we can get a full commitment over a period of time. The following are some prerequisites to having this work the way it should:

- Technology

- Current accounting of all transactions

- Commitment by management

- Buy-in by staff

- Changes in data collection and recording

- Data analytics

Let's take a sec and focus on that last bullet to shed light on the term. Data analytics is the process of examining large and complex data sets to uncover hidden patterns, correlations, and other insights that can be used to make better business decisions. It involves using statistical and quantitative methods to analyze data, identify trends and patterns, and develop predictive models. In short, data analytics is the science of the flash report.

We want to get our clients to a place where they can do a daily accounting of transactions. Technology makes this easier and easier, but it is still not necessarily easy. As technologies come online, there are more efficient ways, as an example, to sync bank accounts to QuickBooks or to the Peachtree, etc. This daily accounting of all transactions is often a significant stumbling block for clients. The best way to approach that topic is gradually over time. In order to get from where the client is today to daily accounting of all transactions, we may need to give ourselves six months or even a year to get there. This daily accounting takes a strong commitment by management, but imagine a business that closes its books every day. Through the lens of the Dimension 1 financial reporting process OKR, this is nirvana.

If senior leadership is open and committed, using flash reports will transform their understanding of the business. This will eventually lead to buy-in by the staff and reinforce the evolution to weekly and even daily accounting. The business will need to up their game about when and how data is collected and recorded, and this takes time. It's tied to the need for technology, which has revolutionized data collection and reporting. You need the support of both the leadership and the staff because unfortunately people hate change, and there is likely to be some resistance. Stay with it.

You should expect resistance, especially from the accounting team because you are going to change their environment. They will not want to change their customary or historical methods of accounting, but what you're helping to implement is a much more efficient way to manage the business. Funny thing is—and you should help them come to this conclusion—it really doesn't change the number of transactions and should not change the amount of time they devote. It's not about what, it's about how. It's simply a change in process and priorities. You'll need to work carefully to get buy-in from the staff with leadership's assistance and cooperation. This amounts to a change in the way data is collected and recorded. If you are going to get to the point where you can collect KPIs in real time, you are going to have to be able to collect the data and be able to export that data in real time on a weekly basis.

What we have found when we convert the systems to daily accounting is enormous satisfaction from senior leadership. It completely changes the way they look at accounting because it makes accounting immediately useful and relevant. Before implementing flash reports, what happens in most of these businesses is that by the time they get the financials, it can be a month or more after the relevant month. The data is stale, not actionable, and has very little use or relevance to what is going on in the business today. By the time they get around to investigating the issues using traditional systems, they are two and a half months out, and the numbers have little utility to leadership going forward.

Side note: Here's another prevalent issue. Historically, most businesses tend to approve transactions after the order has been received. This has to change. Clients shouldn't have to chase invoices, POs, and orders around the building, trying to figure out where they are before they get recorded. That's inefficient and just delays the process. You are going to help them change. Transactions should be approved *prior* to committing to the transaction. This is a different approach and a more efficient approach so that the documentation should merely be a match of the prior approval and easily processed on a daily basis.

When it comes to getting the CEO's buy-in, start simple and build over time. There are a couple of things that are going to occur. One is that the CEO and senior leaders will become accustomed to, and then rely on, the flash report more than any other report. It also provides an opportunity for you to train the leadership on how to interpret the data, and they will begin discussing the data, collaborating on the data, and being accountable to the data. As we mentioned before, the training process builds a new relationship among the leadership team and puts you in a position where you are the go-to person about the report. Once familiar with a given flash report, you will get a clear understanding of where the business is within one minute of getting the report. There are certain benchmarks you expect to meet. As long as everything is hitting what you expect, then the client is fine. If not, you are on the phone talking to the CEO.

CONNECTING FLASH REPORTS AND OKRs

There is a connection between the flash report and the OKRs. As an example, let's think about Dimension 1 again. To refresh, the Dimension 1 OKRs are:

1. Effective Senior Leadership

2. People: Productive and Loyal

3. High Percentage of Recurring Revenues

4. Strong Margins

5. Strong Financial Reporting Processes

6. Scalable Sales Process

7. Strong SOPs

8. High Customer Satisfaction

A lot of what we are measuring here should be on the flash report. As we start tracking these and watching the weekly trends, and as we are doing a rolling thirteen-week forecast (think of it as a rolling quarter), then you are shining a spotlight on the successes and the problems. Here is a great starting point for a flash report tracking twelve metrics:

	Tracked Performance:	Week: Current	Week -1	Week -2	Week -3	YTD
1	Gross Revenue	$230,769.23	$228,461.54	$226,176.92	$223,915.15	$2,727,968.54
2	Net Income	$16,846.15	$16,509.23	$15,848.86	$15,833.01	$195,111.78
3	Net Margin %	7.30%	7.23%	7.01%	7.07%	7.20%
4	Cash Flow: Positive (Negative)	-$12,752.00	-$8,792.00	-$23,761.00	-$8,617.04	-$4,775.99
5	Net Promoter Score	7.6	7.5	7.4	7.4	89.8410972
6	Sales Pipeline Value	$320,000.00	$304,000.00	$297,920.00	$297,324.16	$3,657,732.48
7	Marketing Qualified Leads	372	368	365	361	4,397
8	Recurring Revenues as % of GR	26.00%	25.74%	25.48%	25.23%	25.61%
9	Ratio Cash Actual/Budget, %	83.00%	82.17%	81.35%	80.53%	81.76%
10	Sprints Progress: Red/Yellow/Green	Green, Yellow, Yellow	Green, Green, Yellow	Green, Yellow, Yellow	Yellow, Yellow, Red	Yellow
11	AP	$21,080.00	$19,815.20	$19,022.59	$18,147.55	$234,196.03
12	AR	$64,970.00	$64,905.03	$55,169.28	$39,721.88	$674,298.55

Here is the same flash report, cross referencing the three dimensions of business growth OKRs:

	Tracked Performance:	Week: Current	Week -1	Week -2	Week -3	YTD	Growth-Drive OKR (Needs):	Contributes to (Feeds):
1	Gross Revenue	$230,769.23	$228,461.54	$226,176.92	$223,915.16	$2,727,068.54	Fin: Financial & Operating Reports	Dimension 1 Launchpad
2	Net Income	$16,846.15	$16,509.23	$16,848.88	$15,833.01	$195,111.78	Fin: Financial & Operational Reports; Strong Margins	Dimension 1 Launchpad
3	Net Margin %	7.30%	7.23%	7.01%	7.07%	7.20%	Fin: Financial & Operational Reports; Strong Margins	Dimension 1 Launchpad
4	Cash Flow: Positive (Negative)	-$12,752.00	-$6,792.00	-$23,761.00	-$6,617.04	-$4,775.99	Fin: Financial & Operational Reports	Dimension 1 Launchpad
5	Net Promoter Score	7.6	7.5	7.4	7.4	99.6410972	High Customer Satisfaction; Strong SOP	Dimension 1 Launchpad
6	Sales Pipeline Value	$320,000.00	$304,000.00	$297,920.00	$297,324.16	$3,667,732.46	Scalable Sales Process	Dimension 1 Launchpad
7	Marketing Qualified Leads	372	368	365	361	4,397	Scalable Marketing Process	Dimension 2 Growth
8	Recurring Revenues as % of GR	26.00%	25.74%	25.48%	25.23%	25.61%	High Percentage of Recurring Revenue	Dimension 1 Launchpad
9	Ratio Cash Actual/Budget, %	83.00%	82.17%	81.35%	80.53%	81.76%	Fin: Budget, Forecast, Actuals	Dimension 2 Growth
10	Sprints Progress: Key Result 1 Red-Yellow-Green	Yellow	Green	Green	Yellow	Green	Strategic Vision, Planning, & Execution	Dimension 2 Growth
11	Sprints Progress: Key Result 1 Red-Yellow-Green	Green	Green	Yellow	Red	Yellow	Strategic Vision, Planning, & Execution	Dimension 2 Growth
12	AP	$21,085.00	$19,815.20	$19,022.59	$18,147.55	$234,195.03	Fin: Financial & Operating Reports; Strong SOP	Dimension 1 Launchpad
13	AR	$64,970.00	$64,905.03	$55,169.26	$39,721.88	$674,299.55	Fin: Financial & Operating Reports; Scalable Sales Process; Strong SOP; High Percentage of Recurring Revenue	Dimension 1 Launchpad

NOTES:

Dimension 1 Launchpad	Using flash reports contributes to Effective Senior Leadership
Dims 1, 2 & 3	Business-wide transparency of the flash report contributes to: People: Productive & Loyal, Strategic Culture, Innovation as a Competitive Advantage, and High Growth Compared to Market
Dimension 3 Transferable Value	A history of flash reports allows the business to communicate performance inside and outside, and can create confidence in past and projected performance

This chart links the flash report entries with OKRs. The business may need to reach relevant OKRs before it can effectively track the metric; no matter. Create and implement a first-pass flash report anyway and consistently hold the senior team accountable to generating accurate, timely data. Doing so creates accountability and collaboration and eventually reliance on the report as a management tool. Some smaller businesses may not initially have the data, so there is likely a period of time where that needs to be sorted out. Keep in mind that the flash report above has twelve points, so we know a lot about the business, but you can begin with a simpler flash report. The key is that we are starting to live in our numbers, and that is a habit that the business needs to get into. For instance, in the above flash report, we see a negative cash flow of almost $13,000. We need to know why.

What you are doing here is creating accountability. Remember: One senior leader is accountable for each line on the flash report because if more than one person is accountable, then really no one is accountable. We are also promoting collaboration among senior leaders and among teams while helping change the business culture and mindset. This is a key feature of implementing a flash report. You may face resistance at first, but once they accept that flash reports are a permanent part of the business, and they start to see and discuss what they learn from the flash report, it will become an important tool for creating and maintaining a strategic culture. The report becomes the embodiment of strategic doing.

INITIAL FLASH REPORT

Let's use the initial flash report as a teaching opportunity. Rather than waiting six months to get a flash report, get one started immediately. That way you can start to build a relationship with leadership. In a very short time, they will be telling you what is on the flash report—and they will rely on it. It changes the whole operation and how people manage the business. You can really gain tremendous credibility and enormous buy-in from leadership as well, and they will get very confident not only in the data, but also in you as their guide and advisor.

Meeting with the senior leadership team to go over the flash report gives you an opportunity to train them about interpreting the data. By starting simple and reporting on data that is easy to find, you will start to build leadership's confidence. You will have the opportunity to interpret the data—the condensed cash flow, the cash balance, the deposits, the payables paid, the payroll paid, and the end-of-week balance. You have four weeks of data across the page. It's an instantaneous analysis, especially of what is going on with cash flow. Then you can take each one of those lines and start to train on where this information came from and how to improve data quality and timeliness. Now leadership is getting real-time information on the cash flow of their business on a four-week basis, and they will start to save these flash reports. Next, they can move to eight weeks of condensed accounts receivables, where you have the beginning balance, their sales, their collections, their write-offs, and their adjustments in the end-of-the-week balance. If they are doing daily accounting, then they should be recording sales on a daily basis as well. This is another reason we argue that a top-rated CRM, when kept accurately, is as important as the financial management software.

Pro tip: *Always* have a copy of the weekly flash report sent to you. You want to see that flash report at 9:00 a.m. every Monday. If it's not in your email, you are calling the person in charge to find out why. If not, you are driving over and getting this thing resolved with leadership. Getting the report empowers you to take an hour, have a cup of coffee with the CEO, and talk about the flash report. Talk to the CEO every week and meet with them at least once a month. It's an opportunity to discuss not only what is on the flash report, but also many other things that will come up during the discussion.

Launched as you are with the initial report, start to discuss adding key performance indicators (KPIs) toward the end of the first quarter. You can start to talk about what a KPI is, what metrics you can add to the flash report with the intent of building more information for leadership to operate the business, and also start to identify areas where you can improve profit, cash flow, and the value of the business. Ask: "Team, what else would you like to see on this report?" They are going to be a lot more receptive now because they love the data. They begin to understand that they can have KPI metrics that can measure operations or shipping, packaging, or inventory control. With their buy-in, they are going to be more apt to insist the staff cooperate in obtaining this information accurately and timely. As you start to introduce the concept of the KPIs, make a list of them. Explain to leadership what each one means and start to establish a priority list of the information.

Try to always qualify and quantify the benefit associated with achieving the goal. Quantify the gap, the value of achieving a particular goal or achieving a particular KPI benchmark, and help management understand that in relation to the cash flow benefit and the profitability benefit, there is the value of the business benefit. The flash report is actually tracking (and contributing to) growth capacity and value capacity. There may be other things such as retention of employees, recruiting, turnover of customers, and other measurements that you want to quantify so they start to relate. Continue weekly monitoring, meet with leadership every week, continue to add KPIs, prepare a plan of action to improve performance. Here are two scenarios. In one, you initially identify and point out an area that is weak where you can improve value and suggest that you would like to devise a plan of action to improve performance. It's a problem in a vacuum. In the other scenario, you have six months of flash reports, built their confidence, built the information, and they trust and rely on it. They look at you as a go-to person. Which is better for the client? Which is better for you and your advisory business? You will have measured the area that can be improved and identified how much it is worth. Now you can help them craft a plan that will actually improve performance, and it will be much better received because it came from them, from their discussion, and from their collaboration. This is how a project becomes a multiyear engagement. Continue your weekly contact,[38] education, monitoring sprints, and shepherding execution leadership.

---

38 It's a great idea to keep getting the weekly flash report even if you are no longer engaged with the client. The CEO should see that having your experienced eye on the report might catch things they miss and might clear up issues before they become profound.

CREATING TRANSPARENCY AND ACCOUNTABILITY

While you can start relatively simply, as we get into Dimension 2 we need to really monitor cash, and more importantly we need to *forecast* the cash needed to run the business. While the list of KPIs can vary, one goal is universal: adding a thirteen-week rolling forward cash flow forecast. Thirteen weeks is a quarter. Rolling forward means there are always thirteen weeks on the cash flow forecast. As we complete a week, we add the thirteenth week to the end of the forecast. This presents an opportunity to interpret, monitor, consult, and advise how we can improve the cash flow and anticipate the needs of the business as opposed to reacting to emergencies.

As you protect cash flow and connect it to recurring revenue, consider *not* extending credit to customers without even thinking about their credit worthiness. This avoids waiting thirty, sixty, ninety days after they do not pay to start collection. A better approach would be to establish a credit limit and monitor it. Implement credit holds as soon as they hit the credit limit *before* you accept new orders. Communicate terms of payment in writing and start collection efforts within twenty-four hours of the past-due date. This changes the paradigm of how you manage accounts receivable and inventory. This is where you can find cash the fastest.

Let's look at another area where you need to make the gears of the engine mesh. In shortening the sales cycle, which is part of measuring a salesperson's productivity, examine the closing ratio backlog as well. By the end of year one or two, you want to be able to tie order entry all the way through to shipping and collection so that when an order is entered, you are collecting the data needed by every department. It is automatically funneling through to all the departments, giving them a heads-up about what's coming. Sales says to all, "Here's an order that's going to be processed on x date." Ops knows they need to have the inventory, the supplies, and the labor to get it out, and finance knows they'll need to bill it. It's a wonderful thing. Seems logical, yet few clients do it.

When you put KPIs and flash reports in place, you achieve both leadership buy-in and a collaborative effort among all the departments. Think about the last few clients with whom you worked. In many businesses there are walls between departments, right? They do not work together, and they point fingers when there's a hiccup (so clearly not effective senior leadership). There's a somewhat toxic environment with tribal fiefdoms. Conversely, when you have open-book leadership that uses the flash report and cascades information down to the employee level for people to see, then every single individual realizes an action they take has an effect on performance, cash flow, profit, and value. Having the big numbers displayed on the factory floor, where on the wall are published the goals and objectives of the business, creates an awareness that everyone is working toward the same goal.

Flash reports contribute to Dimension 1's effective senior leadership with collaboration and accountability This launchpad leads into the three dimensions as the flash report should be shared. Get the client to see the value in transparency. This is not a small task: It's often hard to get the CEO to start sharing information, to be transparent. They need to see the power of transparency. You might point out one terrific example of the power of transparency: public companies. You can learn an incredible level of detail about a public company through their SEC filings. If they can be publicly transparent and thrive, it stands to reason that it's not dangerous to have transparency, especially inside the business circle of trust.

One final suggestion: Include a green/yellow/red execution tracker in the report. Sure, the flash report is tracking weekly performance of the business. But what about the strategic initiative, the sprints that are increasing strategic capacity? Shouldn't these be tracked and discussed by the senior team on a weekly basis? You bet they should. Something as simple as green/yellow/red on progress tracks progress of executing the strategic growth project plan.

- Green: Sprint to the key result is on time and to spec.

- Yellow: Sprint to the key result has a delay on time and/or to spec.

- Red: Sprint to the key result has showstopping issues on time and/or to spec.

In addition to giving you, the advisor, a heads-up that all is not well with execution, imagine the conversation during the weekly senior leadership meeting. The CEO can immediately ask why yellow, why red, and the team can discuss causes and solutions. They can instantly collaborate to clear the bottleneck.

Business-wide transparency through the flash report contributes to people: productive and loyal, strategic culture, innovation as a competitive advantage, and high growth compared to the market. These growth-driving objectives will flow from the flash reports. You start tracking growth capacity in Dimension 1 and add Dimension 2 with budget and forecasting, which all contribute to value capacity in Dimension 3 business story, auditable financials, growth compared to the market, and customer spread. Ultimately these flash reports tell the history of the business. Imagine you and your client sliding a three-ring binder of flash reports across the table to a potential buyer. It is a powerful image as the company's story is there in KPIs and dollars.

If the client refuses this transparency, you then need to have the difficult conversation about how committed they are to having the business move forward. This goes back to chapter 1 and the growth conversation, asking good questions, and determining if you still have a committed client. Ask them why they are reluctant and/or what they are worried about. Then when you have their answers, you can think about what to do about it.

One perspective that may have the CEO understand the harm of *not* being transparent is to explain to them that without vetted information, employees will fill in their own answers, and the CEO may not like those answers. It's human nature to fill information voids with voodoo. If they want their employees to fill in the correct information, they need to be the source of that info. Shared information builds teams. Think of a football team with a QB calling plays or a scoreboard. Ultimately, either your client fills in the blanks or the employees will.

> **If they want their employees to fill in the correct information, they need to be the source of that info.**

This brings us full circle: Who is the perfect client? As we qualify clients, we ask questions about how open they are to learning growth, transparency, etc. You need to ask yourself if *you* want to work with clients that have control issues or if you want to focus your energy on clients who have a growth mindset and a transparency mindset. This gets back to proper client mindset fleshed out during the growth conversation. Explain to your potential client that you only work with clients who are open and committed. If you agree that flash reports are transformative, you need to know from the get-go growth conversation that this CEO is willing to be transparent. You need to start discovery already thinking about execution.

RECAP

This chapter discusses the importance of tracking and benchmarking key performance indicators (KPIs) in order to improve business performance. The use of benchmarks helps to set goals and monitor progress toward achieving them. Growth drivers use flash reports as a deeply impactful leadership tool for providing real-time financial information and identifying areas of concern. The objective of using flash reports is not only to help manage the business but also to build a consulting relationship with the client. The report should ideally be on one page and include KPIs to monitor progress toward achieving goals. Accountability for each KPI rests with one senior executive. Start simply tracking relevant and easily available data and evolve over time. The flash report can evolve to track execution of the sprints through which the business increases strategic capacity.

10

BRINGING IT ALL TOGETHER

The Execution Leadership System

What is an execution leadership system? This chapter discusses a topic that is referred to by many different names: business operating system (or BOS), execution management system, etc. Consider this: As the business advisor, you are guiding the senior leadership team, teaching them how to collaborate and be accountable—*as a team*—to the shareholder goals. But all too often there is no established system that guides leadership. So we refer to the proven system described below as an execution leadership system (ELS) because it is the system that the CEO and the senior leadership team will use to drive the business forward. They are not *managing* execution, they are *leading* it.

During your client discovery discussions, you will have gained clarity on the existence and status of the business's operating system (if any). A CEO giving orders is not a system, it's a dictatorship and a drag on strategic capacity, especially on value capacity. If you agree that a guiding principle for business advisors is to leave an indelible positive impact on your clients, then helping them install and use a permanent execution leadership system is key.

During the growth conversation, we saw that qualifying a client includes confirming that they have a can-do and will-do commitment to implement and/or improve an execution leadership system. Absence of these commitments limits the probability of engagement success.

Recapping, you can use the following five elements as a guide during your initial client discovery:

1. Do they have a process for establishing priorities, the important things to get done to achieve the company's vision and mission?

2. Is there a standard system for translating priorities into specific actions?

3. Does the business have a meeting rhythm, a cadence of accountability, communication, and alignment?

4. Does the business prepare, share, and discuss a weekly "company scorecard" such as a standing flash report, dashboard, etc.?

5. Best practice: Are they operating the company in a ninety-day world?

Much of what follows has been discussed throughout the book, but as we are now looking at the system in its totality, we should explore each of these in turn.

1. A PROCESS FOR ESTABLISHING PRIORITIES

"When everything is a priority, nothing is." **—Karen Martin**

Through our deep analysis of the business, we have identified the strengths we can leverage and the underperforming areas that are limiting strategic capacity.

The three dimensions of business growth is a holistic methodology for prioritizing an advisory engagement driven by your client's goals. Where many systems establish priorities based on consensus or perhaps by planning backward from the goal, the three dimensions methodology establishes priorities based on building the capacity needed to deliver objectives, which are steps on the path to the goal. This system has a proven record of success.

The growth-drive execution leadership system borrows from the super-successful Agile system, specifically the waterfall of sprints structure. Remember from chapter 8, a waterfall of sprints is simply a planned series of focused efforts where each builds on the last. Think of success pouring down as a cascade, moving from strength to strength, and you have the concept.

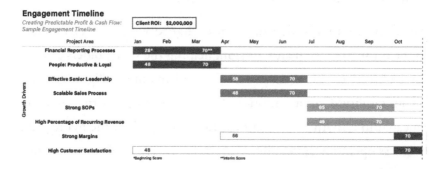

Engagement Timeline
Creating Predictable Profit & Cash Flow: Sample Engagement Timeline

Client ROI: $2,000,000

As part of our discovery during the growth conversation, we gained an initial understanding around "Does this stuff exist?" and "Can this business execute?"

Clients hire us for a reason. For the purposes of this conversation, we are going to assume that, as is the case with so many clients, the very reason we are at the table is that they can't get out of their own way. And it's often the case that CEOs may themselves be the problem with establishing priorities and executing. Note that this is the first area on which we work because the first OKR in Dimension 1 is to create an effective senior leadership team … hence you as the advisor guiding your client as they install and use an execution leadership system.

2. A STANDARD SYSTEM FOR TRANSLATING PRIORITIES INTO SPECIFIC ACTIONS

The OKRs making up the three dimensions are themselves a system for translating priorities into actions. Our job as the advisor, assuming we are working as the architect and general contractor, is to help our CEO hold their team accountable for taking action. Our standard system includes twenty-four growth-driving objectives and their supporting key results.

3. A CADENCE OF ACCOUNTABILITY, COMMUNICATION, AND ALIGNMENT

An effective senior leadership team is aligned with and accountable to the business's vision and mission, helping the shareholders achieve their objectives. How do you create and maintain alignment and accountability? Communication. Communication is structured and repeated in a rhythm of meetings. Take your pick of the many great business operating system books, and there are several constants, one of which is holding regular, effective meetings.

In chapter 3, we discussed senior leadership alignment and how to use a workshop to reach this goal. Becoming an effective workshop and group exercise moderator is a critical skill for business advisors. If you haven't boned up on this, you should. That said, it is not just the senior leadership team that needs to be aligned with and accountable to the shareholders' goals. The entire organization does. Look back at People: Productive and Loyal and Strategic Culture for guidance. You'll note that using the execution leadership system outlined here, you will push alignment and accountability from the boardroom to the shop floor using standing monthly, weekly, and daily communication (meetings). Here's what it looks like:

- Annual two-day off-site strategic planning. The world around us, our market, our competitors, and our strategic capacity to meet challenges and accomplish goals. Attended by senior leadership (plus key direct reports, optional).

- Quarterly alignment and progress; strategic all-day off site. Attended by senior leadership (plus key direct reports, optional).

- Monthly meetings dig deeper into the analyze-design-execute cycle. Two and a half hours on site to discuss where the business is going, where it has gotten to, and what has come up that was not previously expected. What do we think, what do we know, what can we prove? Collaborative discussion creates alignment about what we should do about it. Attended by senior leadership.

- Weekly senior leadership meetings track progress on quarterly goals using the flash report. One and a half hours on site.

- Each individual team also meets weekly, driving transparency deep into the business and keeping pace on KPIs. In the weekly team meeting, the team leader shares company updates and the results from the monthly leadership meeting.

- Daily team huddles: Each team participates in a fifteen-minute daily huddle designed to maintain momentum toward key results.

4. PREPARE, SHARE, AND DISCUSS A WEEKLY SCORECARD LIKE A FLASH REPORT

Businesses run on data. Best-in-class operations track key data—in dollars or otherwise—on a scorecard. We call the scorecard a flash report. It is prepared, distributed, and discussed weekly, without fail. The senior leadership team, not the CEO, contributes to the flash report. One senior leader is accountable for each line on the flash report. For example, the CFO is accountable for tracking revenue and margin, the VP of Revenue is accountable for marketing and sales KPIs, the COO for delivery and customer satisfaction, etc. See chapter 9.

5. OPERATING IN A NINETY-DAY WORLD

The human brain does well with a ninety-day horizon, which ties in nicely with operating in a quarterly world. A business with high strategic capacity is delivering on a multiyear strategic plan. Each year is divided into quarters, months, weeks, and days. You have to break the strategic plan into bites. The execution leadership system relies on a waterfall of sprints to deliver wins.

Here's how it plays out. Think of a three-year engagement whose goal is to deliver a defined transferable value for the business, say $20 million. In each of the three years, you guide the business as it reaches best-in-class objectives for one of the three dimensions of business growth each year. Since there are eight growth-driving objectives per dimension, these split equally for attention into two per quarter. And each objective has an average of six key results. Therefore, in a twelve-week quarter, you can tackle one key result every two weeks.

The OKRs are added to the client's flash report and discussed in weekly meetings. You, the business advisor, design the waterfall of sprints that will deliver key results.

When running at speed, the execution leadership system (ELS) is designed to drive:

1. Two objectives per quarter (eight per year).

2. Over each two-week period, one key result for each of the objectives is brought into line with best practices (four KRs per month).

3. These are listed and tracked in the flash report.

4. One senior leadership team member is assigned accountability for the success of each key result.

It is vital to get some early wins to build morale and confidence. You are the best judge of how much your client can handle. Here are some alternative approaches to launching the ELS: (1) Start with one growth-driving objective for the first quarter; (2) allow four weeks to implement key results; and (3) assign advance prep work, laying the groundwork for upcoming sprints and similar warm-ups as the team gets used to the system. Advance prep can help make up the time used for options one and two. Be creative; the key is to make sure the first sprints are bold yet successful.

In the military there is a preliminary notice by command to staff to subordinate units known as the warning order. A warning order is a preliminary notice of action to follow. The warning order is issued prior to the planning process so subordinate leaders can maximize their prep time. Consider using this same technique as you guide senior leaders in the execution leadership system.

Successful execution depends on increasing strategic capacity. Tools like the CLARITY Strategic Capacity Analysis provide the analysis data for strategic capacity in each of the twenty-four OKRs, making the business easier to run while increasing growth and transferable value.

ESTABLISHING A RHYTHM OF EFFECTIVE MEETINGS

A successful execution leadership system is rooted in effective communication through a repeated rhythm of meetings. If you do nothing else, guide your clients to instituting the weekly and monthly

PRO TIP: Sample agendas and support resources are available through www.growth-drive.com.

meetings using the principles described here. The execution leadership system depends on the constant communication delivered through these meetings for success.

The annual meeting, quarterly meeting, and weekly meetings are *always* held. Monthly meetings are optional when they coincide with quarterly meetings (which are held in the first month of each quarter) and always held in months two and three. If you are struggling with whether to put on a monthly meeting as well as a quarterly, ask yourself if during the two-and-a-half-hour monthly on-site meeting you might swap out potentially duplicative elements and replace them with education or a team-building exercise.

The annual and quarterly meetings focus on strategy and strategic execution. In these meetings, you focus on growth goals and growth-driving objectives; monthly meetings connect strategy and tactics by focusing on key results in the context of growth-driving objectives, and the weekly meeting is all about tactical execution and key results.

The following are example agendas that can be tailored for individual client cases.

THE ANNUAL MEETING:
STRATEGY DEVELOPMENT AND ALIGNMENT

If you are helping the business implement an execution leadership system, you as the business advisor will eventually need to moderate an off-site planning meeting. This meeting is repeated annually. In this meeting the CEO and their senior team will discuss mission, vision, and strategy.

There is a lot of work to be done preparing for the annual meeting, especially so for the first, which is the kick-off of the new execution leadership system. As a well-trained, prepared, and supported business advisor, in the kick-off annual meeting you will literally launch the client team on a path to increasing strategic capacity, through which they will drive growing profits and transferable value. And here too the data is in: Executing a plan with accountability almost guarantees some quick wins and terrific long-term results.

The first annual meeting is the kick-off meeting. This may be the first time that the team has had an experience like you're about to deliver. Remember: the power is in the room, and with your playbook and experience, you will harness this power to the strategic growth plan and start moving the business forward. It's fun and rewarding, as you'll soon see.

The annual meeting is held off site for one to two days (depending on the size of the business and team) at a hotel or similar venue. The advisor and CEO will have enough work without also having to manage the room, food, etc. Attendees are limited to senior leadership and optionally their key top direct reports.

PRO TIP: You can always collaborate with a seasoned pro, a coach, or other moderator who rides shotgun supporting your first meeting.

Here's what an agenda might look like. For those of you who have been through a program like the Growth-Drive Specialist Certification or Business Advisor Mastermind Group, much of this will feel very familiar. You know from firsthand experience how powerful these techniques are.

This agenda assumes that the senior leadership team has completed a senior leadership alignment workshop and is familiar with the three dimensions of business growth's twenty-four growth-driving objectives. If not, workshop the concepts with them.

Before the retreat, participants are given the agenda, plus some homework, including the need to prepare for discussions and exercises (see "Prep" notation).

There are several great resources you can also study when planning these meetings. The giants are of course the works of Verne Harnish and Gino Wickman, which are referenced in the Growth-Drive Playbook.

The kick-off and subsequent annual meetings require follow-up, during which you will be creating or updating the execution leadership system. You should be asking yourself: "How do I keep up the momentum and excitement that we created during the off site?" Here are a couple of ideas:

1. Upgrade their weekly team meetings by introducing the flash report and assigning accountabilities among the team. Remember, start simple.

2. Generate, track, and celebrate some early wins. Early wins can be changes in behavior and examples of increased collaboration. Identify and highlight for all an experience, process, or result that has changed from bad to good, etc. With your ear to the rail, you will pick up these nuggets. It's your job as the business advisor to prompt folks to share and celebrate these in weekly and daily meetings.

QUARTERLY MEETINGS: STRATEGIC DEVELOPMENT, STAYING ON PACE BUILDING STRATEGIC CAPACITY, GROWTH ACTION CYCLE PHASES ANALYZE & DESIGN

The quarterly meeting is a full-day off site. This meeting focuses on strategic capacity and ninety-day progress toward the annual goals. The quarterly meeting ties the monthly meetings to the annual meeting.

It's a judgment call driven by factors including the size and sophistication of the senior team as to whether to hold both an annual and a quarterly meeting. The same comment is true about quarterlies and monthlies. The bigger the organization, the more moving parts and the more time is needed to create alignment and accountability. Some ideas for swapping out meeting modules are discussed in the subsequent section.

Full-Day, Off Site; in addition to or replacing monthly meeting

After this meeting, the senior leadership team will agree on
and be accountable to the coming quarter's goals and will
have a common list of updates to be communicated to their
teams (and thereby throughout the organization).

-Focus is on goals and strategy

-Create/confirm actions toward key results and growth-driving objectives

-Define accountabilities, time bound

-Accountabilities each assigned to one senior leader

-Use action board and parking lot

-Action board clearly spells out communication points for teams

Materials: writing pads, pens, plus two Post-it easels, and markers.

10 mins	Welcome, housekeeping, present agenda	CEO and Business Advisor
10 mins	Check-in exercise, all participants	Business Advisor
10–20 mins	Strategic Culture: roundtable shout-out about behaviors bringing guiding principles to life	Open mic
60 mins	Goals, mission, and strategy discussion	Moderated by CEO and Business Advisor
10 mins	Group: celebrate quarterly wins and other good news	Open mic
10 mins	Break	
60 mins	Previous quarter goals, objectives, and performance	A senior leader (not CEO) assigned to lead, round-robin
20 mins	Group Discussion: What went well, where can we improve?	Moderated by Business Advisor
60 mins	Break: lunch and free time (brain break)	Suggest all discuss previous session in small groups over lunch

150–180 mins	This quarter's objectives: increasing strategic capacity. Presentation and discussion. Stop for a recap and/ or get people physically moving at ninety minutes.	Led by Business Advisor or trained senior leader (standing assignment)
10 mins	Break	
30 mins	Where are we on the path to executing our annual plan?	Led by Business Advisor or trained senior leader (standing assignment)
30 mins	Key takeaways and accountabilities	CEO and Business Advisor

MONTHLY MEETING: STRATEGIC PROGRESS, GROWTH ACTION CYCLE PHASES ANALYZE AND DESIGN

Monthly meeting: two and a half hours, on site. Agenda: Where are we going, where have we gotten to, what has come up that we didn't expect? What do we think, what do we know, what can we prove? Monthlies are attended by the senior leadership team, who uses the weekly team meetings to connect this strategic meeting with tactical execution.

The monthly meeting is in addition to the weekly meeting. The CEO's role is to learn and ask questions: This is a meeting of an effective senior leadership team. The Business Advisor should attend and help moderate.

Focus is on strategy and tactics, growth-driving objectives, plus touching on key results.

Keep the team aligned and grow them as leaders.

Review and discuss performance against quarterly plan.

Maintain momentum by celebrating wins.

Reinforce collaborative accountability.

Remember: This same group is working with the flash report in the standing weekly meeting.

Assumes three to eight senior leaders. Two and a half hours.

5 mins	Check-in exercise: number and what's good personally and professionally?	Monthly round-robin
60 mins	Education: business advisor or outside expert on a topic relevant to the team's journey, or ask one of the senior leaders to present a case based on internal experiences or outside ideas/best practices	Business Advisor, outside expert or senior leader
5 mins	Break	
5 mins	Company update: state of the business, focusing on strategic culture and capacity	Monthly round-robin
30 mins	Progress on quarterly goals: Presentation and discussion. Where are we winning?	A senior leader (not CEO) assigned to lead, round-robin
30 mins	Leadership roundtable: issue-resolution exercise. Where are we stuck? Promote collaboration to get unstuck.	Led by Business Advisor or trained senior leader (standing assignment)
15 mins	Key takeaways and accountabilities	CEO and Business Advisor

WEEKLY MEETINGS: FOCUS ON TEAM-LEVEL TACTICAL EXECUTION, GROWTH ACTION CYCLE "EXECUTE"

The CEO's role in the weekly meeting is to ask questions. They should say little and expect much. Coach the CEO about constructive communication techniques: lots of why, how can we do better, what else should we have tried, how can we leverage this win, etc.

As we discussed earlier in the book, we are focused on creating a collaborative rather than simply a collegial team. This mantra shared by a senior

> "The most important team is the one you are on, not the one that you lead."

pro during their certification workshop is right on point: "The most important team is the one you are on, not the one that you lead."

Agenda guidance for weekly meetings:

- Role of the CEO: call the meeting to order, briefly. Listen and ask clarifying questions with a light touch, but do not dominate the meeting. This is a senior leadership meeting, not a CEO meeting. Saying less leaves accountability and collaboration with the team.

- Walk through the flash report, with each accountable team member updating the team about progress on their line item(s).

- In the flash report, track and discuss progress on OKR sprints, which are tagged green/yellow/red using quantitative criteria:

- Green: on track for completion on time and to spec.

- Yellow: moving forward but not on track to be completed on time and/or to spec. The accountable senior leader should be prepared to explain why and ask for help from the team. This is not a place to assign blame, this is an opportunity to promote collaboration and collective, systemic problem solving.

- Red: stalled. The accountable senior leader should be prepared to explain why (the CEO should be *asking* why) and ask for help from the team.

Pro tip: If you're following best practices, the senior leadership team will have participated in some or all of a Senior Leadership Alignment Workshop, the annual kick-off, and in ongoing quarterlies and monthlies. They should therefore have a good grasp on the strategic growth plan, growth-driving objectives, and the concept of key results and sprints, making the weekly meetings smooth and productive.

Here they are tracked in the flash report:

	Tracked Performance:	Week: Current	Week -1	Week -2	Week -3	YTD	Growth-Drive OKR (Needs):	Contributes to (Feeds):
1	Gross Revenue	$230,799.23	$228,461.54	$226,176.92	$223,915.15	$3,727,968.54	Fin: Financial & Operating Reports	Dimension 1 Launchpad
2	Net Income	$16,846.15	$16,509.23	$15,846.86	$15,833.01	$195,111.78	Fin: Financial & Operational Reports; Strong Margins	Dimension 1 Launchpad
3	Net Margin %	7.30%	7.23%	7.01%	7.07%	7.29%	Fin: Financial & Operational Reports; Strong Margins	Dimension 1 Launchpad
4	Cash Flow: Positive (Negative)	-$12,752.00	-$8,792.00	-$23,761.00	-$8,617.04	-$54,775.99	Fin: Financial & Operational Reports	Dimension 1 Launchpad
5	Net Promoter Score	7.6	7.5	7.4	7.4	86.8410972	High Customer Satisfaction; Strong SOP	Dimension 1 Launchpad
6	Sales Pipeline Value	$320,000.00	$304,000.00	$297,920.00	$297,324.16	$3,657,732.46	Scalable Sales Process	Dimension 1 Launchpad
7	Marketing Qualified Leads	372	368	366	361	4,397	Scalable Marketing Process	Dimension 2 Growth
8	Recurring Revenues as % of GR	26.00%	25.74%	25.49%	25.23%	25.61%	High Percentage of Recurring Revenue	Dimension 1 Launchpad
9	Ratio Cash Actual/Budget, %	83.00%	82.17%	81.35%	80.53%	81.76%	Fin: Budget, Forecast, Actuals	Dimension 2 Growth
10	Sprints Progress: Key Result 1 Red/Yellow/Green	Yellow	Green	Green	Yellow	Green	Strategic: Vision, Planning, & Execution	Dimension 2 Growth
11	Sprints Progress: Key Result 1 Red/Yellow/Green	Green	Green	Yellow	Red	Yellow	Strategic: Vision, Planning, & Execution	Dimension 2 Growth
12	AP	$21,060.00	$19,815.20	$19,022.59	$18,147.55	$234,195.03	Fin: Financial & Operating Reports	Dimension 1 Launchpad
13	AR	$64,970.00	$64,905.03	$55,169.26	$39,721.86	$674,298.95	Fin: Financial & Operating Reports; Scalable Sales Process; Strong SOP; High Percentage of Recurring Revenue	Dimension 1 Launchpad

NOTES:

Dimension 1 Launchpad	Using flash reports contributes to Effective Senior Leadership
Dims 1, 2 & 3	Business-wide transparency of the flash report contributes to: People: Productive & Loyal, Strategic Culture, Innovation as a Competitive Advantage, and High Growth Compared to Market
Dimension 3 Transferable Value	A history of flash reports allows the business to communicate performance inside and outside, and can create confidence in past and projected performance

The weekly meeting is held every Monday (or the first business day) and never skipped. Ninety minutes on site. If the CEO is absent, the team runs the meeting themselves.

Who should attend? The CEO's leadership direct reports. As with the monthly meetings, this is a leadership meeting, not a CEO meeting. The CEO should say little and should only ask questions. An effective senior leadership team can run the business smoothly in the CEO's absence. The conduct of the weekly meeting is where this should be most evident.

Here's the agenda; it's the same every week. As the business advisor, three things should be true:

1. You receive an email of the flash report every Monday by 9:00 a.m. local.

2. You have a standing fifteen-minute check-in call with the CEO after the meeting each week. The flash report plus this quick chat will keep your finger on the pulse. You should also periodically drop in for coffee with the CEO in lieu of this call.

3. You have standing open office hours that the senior team can use to check in with you one on one. If they don't call you, consider calling them.

	Assumes three to eight senior leaders. Each gets the flash report before the meeting. Ninety minutes max.	
5 mins	Check-in exercise: number and what's good personally and professionally?	Weekly round-robin
5 mins	Celebrate: company-wide good news	Open mic
20 mins	Flash Report Review: highlight wins, identify issues	Round-robin
5 mins	Prioritize top three flash issues for discussion, by consensus	CEO leads
30 mins	Flash issues discussion (10 mins per)	Group discussion moderated by CEO through Q/A
15 mins	Performance against quarterly plan: dollars and KPIs	Group discussion led by a senior leader other than the CEO, standing assignment
10 mins	Key takeaways and accountabilities. CEO-led.	CEO-led

DAILY HUDDLE: MICRO-TACTICAL TRACKING, GROWTH ACTION CYCLE EXECUTE

The daily huddle is where the rubber meets the road, where the execution leadership system comes to life on the shop floor. Managers have assigned tasks that build toward reaching or maintaining a key result, and during the daily huddle, they are making sure that the team is on pace. The green/yellow/red system works well here. The author has found that these are most effective when run literally as a "standing" meeting, not in a conference room but standing in a common area. The daily huddle must identify bottlenecks to progress, and the team should discuss and collaboratively decide on a plan to quickly neutralize these bottlenecks. Bottlenecks are a normal symptom of progress. The daily huddle is also a powerful forum for quick collaboration and wins shout-outs—end the huddle on a high note.

RECAP

An execution leadership system focuses on making goals reality. The ELS establishes goals and prioritizes the tasks needed to achieve the goal. The ELS is rooted in communication. The mechanism for communication is the meeting. An effective business leadership system relies on a rhythm of meetings to communicate past performance and future objectives. If the business advisor only does one thing to ensure they are helping to drive growth, it is establishing the monthly and weekly meetings.